PRAISE FOR *BREA*...

"This is a deeply meaningful book about life and faith. Compelling, moving, and beautifully written, it will touch your heart and deepen your faith."

—*ADAM HAMILTON*, LEAD PASTOR OF UNITED METHODIST CHURCH OF THE RESURRECTION, AUTHOR OF *PREPARE THE WAY FOR THE LORD*

"What do you do when you come to the end of yourself, when your life isn't turning out how you had planned it? We've all been there and yet this is often where Jesus finds us and makes us whole again. My friend Jacob Armstrong is a wise and patient guide, walking us through his own seasons of despair and pain, pointing us to the One who bore our sorrows. If you need rest for your weary soul, if your heart is heavy with hopelessness, this book will be like a cup of fresh water. Read it and see if God will meet you in its pages."

—*DANIEL DARLING*, DIRECTOR OF THE LAND CENTER FOR CULTURAL ENGAGEMENT, COLUMNIST, BESTSELLING AUTHOR OF SEVERAL BOOKS, INCLUDING *THE CHARACTERS OF CHRISTMAS*, *THE CHARACTERS OF EASTER*, AND *THE DIGNITY REVOLUTION*

"Pastor Jacob is a friend. We probably don't agree on everything theologically, but we share a mutual conviction that Jesus is a precious help to those suffering in the throes of affliction and pain. In *Breaking Open*, he shares biblical wisdom for understanding how God not only is near to us in our pain but uses it in remarkable ways to shape our lives for his glory."

—*ERIK REED*, LEAD PASTOR OF JOURNEY CHURCH, PRESIDENT OF KNOWING JESUS MINISTRIES, AUTHOR OF *UNCOMMON TRUST*

"The common denominator of humanity is pain. We all hurt. Sometimes it surfaces as an acute heartache, or as a lingering anxiousness, or as the consequence of a tragedy. And yet sometimes it seemingly appears out of nowhere. During my darkest seasons of grief, I turn to a basic prayer, a phrase as full of questions as it is full of faith: "God, just don't leave me *alone*." Jacob is attuned to the aches of living and his words provide a knowing companion as we lament what we have lost and yearn for new life ahead. These words kindle hope and a thread of belief that God is indeed near to those breaking open."

—*ANDREW GREER*, SINGER/SONGWRITER, AUTHOR OF *TRANSCENDING MYSTERIES*, COHOST OF THE PODCAST *DINNER CONVERSATIONS WITH MARK LOWRY AND ANDREW GREER*

BREAKING

OPEN

BREAKING

OPEN

HOW YOUR PAIN BECOMES
THE PATH TO LIVING AGAIN

JACOB ARMSTRONG

W PUBLISHING GROUP

AN IMPRINT OF THOMAS NELSON

ISBN 978-0-7852-5832-2 (TP)
ISBN 978-0-7852-5854-4 (eBook)
ISBN 978-0-7852-5941-1 (audiobook)

Library of Congress Control Number: 2021952567

Printed in the United States of America
22 23 24 25 26 LSC 10 9 8 7 6 5 4 3 2 1

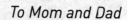

To Mom and Dad

CONTENTS

BREATHING
AND CRYING

Our first breath was a cry.

We have laughed. We have cheered.

We have praised, encouraged, complimented.

With the same mouth we have questioned, criticized, ridiculed, and cursed. (You kiss your mama with that mouth?)

We have whispered.

We have unintentionally raised our voices.

Some of us have been trained to sing. Some have fought hard not to stutter.

Some of us remember a moment when we found our voice. Some remember when our voice strangely changed. Some of us have done that helium thing one too many times.

We have made a lot of different sounds for a lot of different reasons (sounds out of our *mouths*—stay focused).

We voice many different utterances over the course of a day. And there have been hundreds of hours in our lives when we have not made a peep.

But our first breath was a cry.

It was the same for all of us. Before we ever learned a word in our native language, we all shared the same native cry. An appeal for help. A sound of desperation. Or was it fear? Or was it just a sound to say, *This is quite a lot to take in in one moment*?

We were greeted by our loved ones: "Welcome to the world!" Our response? We wept.

If at your birth you didn't cry, there was someone there hoping you would cry, who then helped you to cry. Why?

The first cry of a newborn baby is a kickstart to the lungs. It prepares you for a world where you've got to know how to breathe, and you've got to know how to cry.

It's funny that, even when we've moved well past infancy, the emphasis on breathing remains and we usually do it without even noticing, while the importance of crying seems to lessen as we age.

This book isn't about learning to cry. It is about finding your life. That may or may not involve tears for you. I don't know. But it will involve an exercise that is similar to what happened when you breathed your first breath. It will involve an openness to life that is equal parts terrifying and exhilarating. In the same way your first cry was not voluntary, this also may seem like something you don't get to choose.

There is a second birth that happens in our lives. It is often viewed negatively as a breaking point; some even refer to it as breaking down. Some of us spend our adult lives trying to outrun it.

I think our lives are about something much bigger than simply outrunning this breaking. I think life is all about breaking open. Like our first birth moment, our second invitation to life is dramatic, beautiful, and scary. And the only way we are going to keep breathing is if we open our mouths to cry.

That's how it started for me. It started with crying again. And it started with Daniel.

———

I met Daniel in my backyard. In my hammock. With my beagle puppy licking his face.

For weeks, Simon (the beagle) had been mysteriously escaping our fenced-in backyard. I would get calls from the neighbors. There were reports of trash cans turned over. It was a tense time. I couldn't figure it out.

Until one day when I came home early from work and found and met Daniel in the aforementioned hammock, with the escape-artist beagle, both of them quite content with their unauthorized friendship. Daniel was my twelve-year-old neighbor. He sometimes forgot to close the gate behind him.

Daniel became my companion in that season of my life. I was newly married, working as a pastor, and going to school full time. Whenever I was home working in the yard, Daniel was beside me. I remember going on walks with my wife, Rachel, at the end of a long day. We would have just started holding hands and talking about our day when we would realize, by the sound of footsteps behind us or a third shadow on the ground, that Daniel had joined us. I would take a deep breath as I prepared to hear about Daniel's day instead of Rachel's. I found him both endearing and annoying. A movie on the couch, and there would be Daniel's hand in the shared popcorn bowl. A Saturday lunch and Daniel needed a PBJ too. You get the picture. It was not really how I had imagined my first year of marriage. He was an interruption, and we loved him.

One Saturday night in February, I had fallen asleep on the couch and was woken up by a knock on the door. It was Daniel. He was bundled up in a big winter jacket. I invited him in, but he wouldn't move off the welcome mat. I could tell something was wrong. He wasn't as talkative as usual. He wasn't open. Immovable, he stood by the door, shivering. Wiping the sleep from my eyes and my brain, I tried to make sense of this middle-of-the-night moment. We talked for a bit. But I couldn't shake the feeling that something wasn't right.

I encouraged him to go home. No—I *told* him to go home, wake up his dad, and tell him what was going on. But I didn't walk him home. And I didn't call his dad. I went back to sleep. Daniel left my front porch, walked out into a cold night alone, and some time that night took his own life.

When I heard the news of Daniel's suicide, a darkness covered me. It felt like a panic attack at first, but then it settled into my heart and my bones as a deep, deep sadness. The weight of his loss became my new companion. I remember that first night after I heard, staying up all night, lying in bed. I thought that maybe when the sun came through the blinds in my bedroom window I would feel somewhat better. The sun rose, light and warmth filled my room, but my heart still felt cold and empty. I was a twenty-two-year-old seminary student, which means I was studying to be a pastor. I had just made the decision to give my life to helping people. And somehow with Daniel, I had missed it. Shame and regret replaced hopes and dreams. I told God, *If ever I was going to be used for something good, I know I have squandered that now.* This may sound like a lifted line from a biblical character in the Old Testament, but it was really how I felt.

And then I ran away.

I called my brother, who lived in the desert of southern Arizona, and asked if I could come visit. He said yes. He had to work, but he welcomed my short-notice visit if I didn't mind being alone. That worked perfect for me; I didn't want to see anyone anyway. I got on a plane, leaving my wife, who was grieving the same loss as me, to try to figure out how to make it through my first breakdown.

I spent the days visiting with my brother, Andy, and walking the trails in the desert behind his house. He lived at the foot of the Superstition Mountains. It was dry and barren, and that felt just right to me. One day I noticed a particularly striking mountain that looked like a big shelf sticking out of the range and asked my brother about it. He told me its name: the Flatiron. That was the place of isolation I knew I needed to escape to.

The next day I left as a miserable man on a miserable hike. The only pair of shoes I had brought were a pair of Teva sandals, which were not the perfect hiking shoes for the loose rocks and steep inclines of the barely visible desert trail. I watched my feet get covered in dust and sand. Sharp rocks cut my toes and cactus spines scraped my ankles. My aching feet became a step-by-step metaphor for my irritated mind and heart. The grief I felt in Tennessee felt like anger in Arizona. I wanted to yell at the mountain or shake my fist at the sky.

The Superstition Mountains were the result of prehistoric volcanic activity, and I felt a volcano bubbling up in my body. I didn't know how to deal with my sorrow, my regret, my pain. Each step of the hike brought me closer to the breaking I was destined for and probably needed to have.

By midafternoon I had made it to the top. I was completely exhausted. I had packed no lunch, and I sat down at the edge of the big rock like a sad sack. And that's where I said my rehearsed line to God, which I already told you about. *If ever I was going to be used for something good, I know I have squandered that now.* And it was there on the top of the Flatiron, the farthest place I could think to run away from my house of grief, that God met me.

I didn't hear a voice. I didn't see a vision. But I felt God's presence. And I spoke to him again. In a cry.

I cried.

Finally, I cried. I cried like a boy who hadn't cried in a long time. I mean, shrills like a newborn. The sound was so unfamiliar to me at first that I didn't even know I was crying. It just felt like the only way I could breathe in that moment. The only way I could live was if I cried out to God. It was like my body remembered my first gasp for air and how it led to a cry in my mother's arms. The tears pouring out of me were as important to me as the air coming into my lungs. This cry seemed that desperate. If I didn't get it out, I wasn't going to make it.

The volcano of anger erupted into tears of longing for healing and help from a God who had followed me on a flight to Phoenix.

I looked down at my phone. One bar. I had service. I called my brother.

"Hey, Andy, I made it to the top of the Flatiron." I told him I was hurting. I'm sure he could tell that I was crying. He said we would talk, then he asked me, "You realize you have to walk down, right?"

The next day, Andy conveniently had a day off work, and he took me with his two-person kayak to a lake that cut narrow shafts through high rock-face ravines. We talked and paddled. I told him how bad it felt. How bad I felt. We fished. I wasn't good at sharing how I felt. Really, I wasn't good at knowing how I felt. I tried. The casting and the gentle waves seemed to create a rhythm for me to figure out how to talk about what was going on inside. A loving brother's silent presence seemed to shine light on a pathway where I could take my first steps toward healing. I felt like my short breaths of grief were lengthening. I could almost see clearer.

And then a storm came. Unexpectedly. It began to rain, and rain hard. Andy urged me to paddle faster as we tried to reach the shore. We began to laugh as we got soaked by a rare desert rain. I sat in the front of the kayak, my back to my brother, and my laughter turned to tears again. My brother couldn't see—I don't think—that my walled-off heart had just cracked. It was a good thing. I was breaking. But I was breaking open.

I was hurting, but I wasn't alone. I had run away, but I would return. I had squandered, but God had gathered up all the broken pieces. He had noticed me and sought me out in my newfound suffering. Jesus, whom we know as God who came to earth in flesh, became real to me in the pain. He wasn't going to be just the Savior of my youth. He would not remain only an inspiring feeling at a worship service. Jesus, whose hands and ankles were dust-covered and bloodied, was with me in my desert. I thought I was destined to a life of darkness and despair, but instead he was showing me a different way. It was an open way, and I would take it.

These newfound tears were not the sign of my breakdown. Something else was happening. They were kickstarting my heart back to life again.

The cry of our second birth is like the cry of our first. It opens us up to a whole new life with people who love us and people who will fail us. (Spoiler alert: they are the same people.) The tears open us up to life. They open us up to God.

Breakdowns leave us exhausted—even the little ones, like when we are stuck in a traffic jam while running late. They deplete us. So does life. And then we isolate. We give up on hopes and dreams. We lash out. Sometimes, we run away.

But there is a different option. There is another way.

It's harder.

It still involves breaking, but the breaking has a different purpose—a different endgame. This breaking leads to an openness that, amazingly, brings more life. It actually brings real life. Against all odds, it fills us up, leads us closer to God, and moves us forward. It's called breaking open. It's painful, yes. But the pain leads to the path of living again.

one

BREAKING OPEN, NOT BREAKING DOWN

You need not cry very loud; He is
nearer to us than we are aware of.

BROTHER LAWRENCE

Breaking happens when you come to a place where you've just had enough.

You don't feel like you can keep going. You are broken. You are down.

Breakdown.

You're on the ground. Metaphorically, maybe literally.

You're done.

You're toast.

Enough.

First, let me make this clear. This is not a book about how to avoid a breakdown. No way. "Breakdowns come and breakdowns go. So what are you going to do about it? That's what I'd like to know."[1] (Another life-changing moment is listening to Paul Simon's *Graceland* album. I did when I was six years old. Never been the same. Thank you, Dad.)

Breakdowns are a part of life. We all break down from time to time. There are minor breakdowns, like when you have had a long day and have to go to the grocery store after work and someone has fifty-five items in the fifteen-item line (forty too many, sir!). Then there are major breakdowns, like when the business you have built is destined for bankruptcy, and it's more like your dream than your business. There are minor breakdowns that feel major, and there are major breakdowns that we expend a ton of energy convincing ourselves are minor.

If by *breakdown* we mean a moment when we have just had enough and don't feel like we can keep going, then our goal in life should not be to avoid breakdowns. Honestly, we couldn't completely avoid them even if we tried. Our goal is to figure out how to look at them—how to live in them and live after them.

What I want to share with you is not a tried-and-true way to walk through life and avoid bruises and bumps. That is not really living. What I want to share is how your bruises and bumps and breaks are actually a part of the good life that you get to live.

THE HUMAN EXPERIENCE IS ONE OF BREAKING

As a pastor for twenty years for people of different ages, races, and life experiences, I have seen lots of differences in people culturally, financially, and politically. I have witnessed Democrats who live and thrive in red states. I have seen people who typically like traditional worship enjoying a church that has a rocking band. I have seen fans of the University of Alabama happily living in Tennessee—seen it with my own two eyes! But all the people I have had the pleasure to be around, from Nicaragua to Nashville, have one thing that is familiar to them, one shared experience. What we all share is an ache. Everybody I have ever talked to has this same ache. It is a longing. And I feel it too.

Everyone aches to be whole. We ache to be healed. We ache to be restored. Most of the time, though, we wouldn't put it in those words. We just know we are broken because our child is addicted. We ache because the depression of our youth is now the depression of our golden years. We are stretched to the point of breaking because our career ambitions position us to commit to a pace we can't sustain. Miscarriage, divorce, loneliness. In all of it, we ache. We ache for some way to walk through this life and not give up or give in.

That's often where the breaking happens. Sometimes it seems that our only option is a good old-fashioned, on-the-floor meltdown. And I'm not against these. We see some pretty good ones in the Bible that lead to really amazing lives. Nehemiah hit the ground in anguish for days before he rose to rebuild a wall, a city, and a people. Esther almost broke as she faced her wailing uncle, then resisted safe silence and finally spoke up. Saul felt the dust of the Damascus road on his skin before he stood with new eyes to see. We might call those breakdowns, but there was something else happening there too. Something much different. Those moments were the path to living again.

Break open. You see, we will all face breaking points, and many times we will splinter and crack. We all know broken hearts and broken relationships intimately. With Jesus, these are the opportunities not to fall and stay down but to fall and rise differently. To rise with power, with hope, with purpose. We get to rise, open to a new way of living!

To do that, though, we can't avoid the breaking. We can't stuff it down deep under a coping mechanism. We can't outrun it by moving fast enough. We can't numb it with another show, another drink, or another cynical comment. We can't avoid it by manufacturing drama to gain others' attention. Nope. There is only one way to thrive in life, and that is not by shutting down; it's by remaining open.

Jesus encountered brokenness and, instead of using a supernatural force field to hold suffering at bay, he embraced it. Fully. And he himself broke. But Jesus did it in a way that brought healing, that brought others in, and brought life.

Even better still, Jesus invites us to live a healed, whole life as those who break open toward God. That's right. For Jesus this isn't about leading us down a road where we break. He knows the road we are on is broken, so he is leading us to hope, healing, and wholeness.

As we talk about breaking, remember that we are headed to a wide-open space that Jesus is preparing for us, where all the broken places are made whole. And so, we break. We break open to Jesus. We break open toward others instead of seeking the tempting allure of isolation. We break open and live desperate, vulnerable lives that invite others to do the same.

Over the next seven chapters we will look at ways that we commonly seek to avoid breaking—seven ways we avoid the pain and just try to push through. I will show you that these seven ways are stealing life from us. We will walk through a progression of seven Jesus-ways that move us from merely breaking down to breaking open. And the Jesus-ways get us to the good stuff—what he called "more and better life" (John 10:10 MSG).

But we usually start all this tired. Real tired. So tired you might have read the last few paragraphs and not even noticed how good it sounded because all you could think of was the effort required to get going. *Just too tired.* Exhaustion makes it hard for us to focus. It can blur our eyes, fog our minds, and keep us from taking something on, especially something as monumental as our entire lives changing.

And that's why I'm going to ask you to do three things:

1. Let go of the idea that you are going to save yourself.

2. Commit to keep going.

3. Believe that in a moment everything can change for you. (This is also called hope.)

Here's a shorter way of saying this:

1. You have to let go.

2. You have to keep going.

3. You have to hope.

The first one, "You have to let go," means that we are correct when we think we don't have what it takes to save ourselves from the mess and brokenness. If you think that, you are right. Your body is telling you the truth when it says you are too worn down to take this on. So we have to let that go. We have to dismiss the idea that we can overcome on our own and save ourselves. When we are as tired as this life makes us, we have to own up to the fact that without help we are in deep trouble.

That's one reason the "breaking" part of breaking open is so important. Our long-held belief that we are tough enough and strong enough to persevere leads us to the breaking point. Then, we need to break open by admitting that we need help.

Good news: God is here to help.

God has put together a rescue plan for us, and that is why, when we are tired and feel the temptation to push our way through it, we have to let go. This may be new to you, this letting go and asking God to help. You might even have to try it a few times before it begins to feel natural. But long before you can take any steps toward healing in life, you have to release some things to God. And trust. Yes, that's what I'm talking about—trust. An initial trust that God will take care of all the things you really can't take care of. This letting go usually starts with realizing just how tired you are from trying to carry it all.

BURNED OUT AND STILL ON FIRE

The last time I had talked to my friend Nate, he was so tired. Bone tired. He told me he didn't know if he had anything left.

He was eight years in to starting a new organization. He had given his life to it. There had been beautiful successes, but now he was out of gas. It sounded like he might be done.

And then everything caught on fire.

Literally.

The old church building that housed Nate's community outreach organization caught fire in the middle of a snowstorm, and by the time it was over, the historic edifice had been gutted by flames and was boarded up and abandoned.

I met Nate when he was just starting out. He and his wife, Laura, had moved to Nashville on a dream. A crazy dream. Nate believed that life could come back to a neighborhood that had been left behind by a thriving, bustling city. If Nate had been from Nashville, like me, he would have known better. The area of town he had his heart set on had been, for a couple of generations, the hub of drug use, homelessness, and prostitution. But Nate, a young man with one of those long beards and a bright smile, began riding his bike to an old, dying church every day and meeting the neighbors. What he did was so different from what I had ever seen before in the nonprofit-startup world.

Nate didn't have a cell phone; he relied on face-to-face communication with people. Nate didn't have a car; he rode that bike slowly down the neighborhood streets, taking time to wave and to stop to talk with people. Nate didn't set up a clothes closet or a food pantry; he looked to build sustainable ways that folks could find more life. He began the very slow, hard work of community development, and, over time, he and Laura built a vibrant community at that old, empty church.

I joined Nate during his first summer at Trinity Church in East Nashville as he set up a day camp for kids in the neighborhood. Every day I drove in from my very different context in the suburbs, bringing along Mary and Lydia, my nine- and seven-year-old daughters. These were the first steps for Nate to build trust in the community, and he did it by serving children, mothers, and fathers with a good old-fashioned camp that included music, crafts, and lunch. But really it was love. He was serving love. I, along with Mary and Lydia, witnessed Nate go all in and give himself to a group of people who felt largely forgotten by a rapidly growing "it" city that had its mind set on tourism, expansion, and economics.

Eight years later at Trinity Community Commons (Nate's nonprofit housed in the old church building), Nate's team was hosting weekly meals with healthy food grown in gardens around town. People who were used to going through food lines sat at tables with nice plates and china while live music played. During the day the building was filled with kids receiving tutoring, relationships being built, classes on finances, laughter, conversations, and prayer. Outside the building there was always someone throwing a frisbee, someone talking with a new or old friend, and just plain old dignity being restored.

He had done it. Then, the fire in him went out. And then, a fire burned the building.

The timing was terrible. And at the same time, the timing was typical.

When we give ourselves to our dreams, our passions, our God-given callings, it is exhilarating. It is also hard work. It seems to require all of us. But it seems worth it to build a business, or build a family, or build a relationship. Then, not days in, not months in, but years in, as humans with human limitations, we reach a certain point. A breaking point. It is a point where we can't go on—not on our own.

Nate reached that. I serve on the board of directors for his organization. He told us at a board meeting, with his trademark humility and transparency, that he might be done. He definitely needed a break—and not like a weekend off. That's when the building caught on fire.

Why do I say that is typical? Because it happens all the time. A big blowup when a person is burned out is typical. When a fire burns bright for a while, it also dies down. Sometimes only embers remain.

The culmination of Nate's breakdown was dramatic. It was on the local news. Flames billowed out of old stained glass windows. Two fire companies were required to put it out.

Our flame-outs may not be out in the open, but it's no different. When we reach our breaking points, something will happen that is just too much for us to handle. Help will have to be called in, and there will likely be some smoldering rubble when it's over.

It took me a few days to get to talk to Nate after the fire (mostly because he has no phone). But I knew what was happening. Nate was working hard to handle the continuation of operations, he was taking care of neighbors, he was working with insurance companies. And, as I suspected, Nate was still neck-deep in his own breakdown. When I finally talked to him, he told me exactly that. He told me of all that he had been doing and that he had been crying like he had never cried before. He confessed he had acted like a jerk to the people he loved. And he said he was exhausted.

Then he told me a few things that caught my attention: They had moved their operations to another place where people were helping them get on their feet again. Their neighbors, whom Nate had served for years, were now serving him. He told me he was getting counseling for himself and his staff. And then he shared that he was dreaming again—that maybe this fire would lead to the new birth his organization was really needing. Nate said he had been practicing a different kind of meditative breathing to help with anxiety. God was showing him things about himself and his future. And that's when I knew. Nate was breaking open.

He was letting go of some things.

He was going to keep going.

And he was believing that even the two-alarm fire that had burned his building was going to be a moment for new life to come. I could hear it in his voice. He had hope.

As a board member for Nate's nonprofit, I can say that we are all committed to getting him the rest he needs, the support he needs, and to surround him with love. But his resolution to break open rather than just break down is the key to a beautiful future that I still get to wait with him to see.

"Breakdowns come and breakdowns go. So what are you going to do about it? That's what I'd like to know."[2]

PRACTICING THE DELICATE ART OF BREAKING OPEN

Back to the first thing we need to do: let go. We need to let go of some long-ingrained tendencies to try to fix all our messes and heal all our wounds. We need to let go of control. Some of us reading this are really bad at letting go. Some of us wouldn't even know where to start because we have been in charge of our lives for as long as we can remember. So let's start here.

Remember, we have to let go of the idea that we are going to save ourselves. Let go of that first.

Please drop the idea that you are going to get yourself out of this.

Let go and ask God to help you. (I'll wait. Seriously, ask him. I won't go anywhere.)

Second, we have to commit to keep going. That may sound kind of contradictory to my first request for you to let go. It isn't.

You said "let go," and now you are saying "keep going"?

Right. That's what I said.

(This is a fun imaginary conversation we are having.)

Yes! You let go *and* you keep going. The breaking-open path will hold a lot of seeming contradictions. One reason is that life is messy; we won't try to make everything fit into nice categories. But the main reason is that the way of Jesus holds many of these seeming contradictions, what are often called paradoxes. Just look at Mark 10:43–44, where Jesus said, "Whoever wants to be a leader among you must be your servant, and whoever wants to be first among you must be the slave of everyone else" (NLT). Jesus often left people scratching their heads, thinking, *Huh? Come again, Jesus?* I hope that's what we can do! Ask Jesus what he is really saying. Stay with him a bit longer. I'm hoping that instead of just offering ourselves self-care lines that lift us for a moment, we will walk fully down this messy, broken path that is life and engage the real way of hope and healing.

That means you can let go and give your life fully over to God. It also means that you can keep going. Accept responsibility for what you need to do in this moment. There is a part you play—not as Savior but as a willing, intentional participant in your transformation story. So you have to keep going. Breakdowns put us down, and the implication is that we will stay down. Breaking open keeps us going. We break, but we don't stay stuck. We keep going. We keep moving.

———

I mentioned Nehemiah before. He had one of the most notable breakdowns in the Bible. It is found in the book that bears his name in the Old Testament. Nehemiah was living in a very difficult time for his people, the Jews—the people of God. They were living in exile, which means most of the things they held dear had been stripped from them. They had been uprooted from their homes and forced to serve a new king and a new kingdom. They had lost things like family connections, familiar ways of life, and religious patterns. But like most difficult times there were some folks who managed to do okay. Nehemiah was that guy.

In the midst of exile, he was actually prospering. Well, prospering externally at least. He had a good job. He had a prominent position in the kingdom. Sure, the king was not really treating his people well, but the king was treating Nehemiah well. We all have a friend like this. While the COVID pandemic was one of the hardest seasons ever for many people, most of us know that one friend who got the new job or new house or whose kid received a full ride to an Ivy League college. That was Nehemiah. And even amid all the good things in his life, he broke down too! It turned out that Nehemiah's external condition did not mirror his internal one. It took Nehemiah hearing that his people were suffering in Jerusalem for everything to come apart. Things were going well for Nehemiah but not for the people he loved, and that was a great burden to him.

Nehemiah said this in his book: "When I heard these things, I sat down and wept. For some days I mourned and fasted and prayed before the God of heaven" (1:4). He sat down on the ground and cried and mourned and prayed and didn't eat. For some days he did this. If you see me on the ground for some days crying and not eating, you can call it what it is. Breakdown. Nehemiah had a breakdown!

But the only reason we know Nehemiah's story is because he broke open. His mourning and fasting led him closer to God. In fact, everything about Nehemiah's breakdown involved staying open to God. His heart was broken because he knew there were people who weren't safe, weren't well fed, and weren't happy. He didn't see his high position as separating him from the condition of others. It broke him, but it broke him open in a way that led to action.

If Nehemiah had a several-day breakdown in the Persian kingdom four thousand years ago and then just got up the next day and went about his business and forgot about it, then we never would have heard about it. The reason we know anything about Nehemiah is that his breaking led him to get up and keep going in the direction of where God was leading him. Nehemiah ended up doing all kinds of risky, courageous things to save other people. But it all started with his time on the ground.

Talk to any person who has done any great thing that you admire, and you will find there was a moment when everything changed for them. A moment when they decided to keep going and to keep hoping. Nehemiah did some amazing things. He rebuilt the wall around Jerusalem. He stood up against dangerous enemies. He restored the people of God back to health and connectivity. But when Nehemiah's story started, there was so much crying, so much sadness. I think Nehemiah would say, "I never could have done all that had I not let go of my desire to control it all, had I not given everything to God and resolved to keep going."

With my friend Nate, I know someday there will be some beautiful stories that others will be celebrating, and he will say, "Oh, but did I tell you about the fire? Did I tell you about when it all burned down?"

You see what I'm getting at. This moment you are in, this tired moment, is the moment you will refer back to when you tell your story. There will be no doubt in your mind that it wasn't your greatness or your power that led to the beautiful thing, because you would be toast outside if God had not rescued it all and rescued you.

REDEMPTION IN THE BREAKING

We are marking this moment for you and for me—whether this moment for you is the burned-up moment or you are currently in flames! Write today's date down in your journal or somewhere safe. We have to know this moment, be honest about it, even embrace it. And we have to mark it and remember it. It's here that I will begin to ask you to believe in a redemptive moment. *Redemptive* just means saving, to be brought back. I'm asking you to believe there will be a moment when things change for you. When it is all saved. When it is brought back, and you will see how God rescued you. Write down, "I am marking this moment as the one when I believed something good could happen." Document the date and time so you can tell your grandkids about this moment. The moment you cried but also the moment you kept going.

To believe in a redemptive moment is to hope.

Don't give up hope. Don't give up.

At the risk of being too repetitive, I want to urge you on once more:

Let go.

Keep going.

Choose hope.

To break open, remember, you have to do these three things first. Let go. Keep going. Choose to hope. If it helps, set the book down and think about them for a while. Think about what each one might look like for you. This could be an easy moment for a cry to come. Go with it.

What would letting go mean for you? You may already know what you need to let go of. It's usually the thing that you have tried to control the most, and it has only worn you down. It's probably the thing or things that are most precious to you. Yes, these are the things we are called to let go.

I have to let go of determining my child's future, you might think.

Or *Somehow, I have to let go of the tight grip I have on making my marriage perfect.*

I have to loosen my grip on this cancer that I can't heal.

Please let it go. Set it down.

Are you willing to keep going? You have a part to play. Will you simply say, "Today I will keep going"? Rather than break down and stay down, will you resolve to step forward? What that looks like today is us putting one foot in front of the other as we journey together. Please don't give up; don't resolve to stay in this place. Just. Keep. Moving.

Will you believe a moment is coming for you when all the crud you have walked through will be redeemed? Oh, I hope so! I hope you will hope. But you may have to choose it. Hope may not be handed to you; you might have to claim it. Please take hold of it. Hope is essential for breaking open. It is what keeps us going. Tim Keller once said, "We are controlled . . . by what we think will happen later."[3] Our beliefs about the future hold enormous implications for how we act now. So we have to have a hope for later. We will begin to grasp the picture of Jesus' hope for our *laters* but for now, just hope that *better* is coming. That what you are in right now is not all there is. That this is not the end of the story.

I told you about my first breakdown and my first breaking-open moment when my young friend Daniel died of suicide. I told you about that moment on top of the Flatiron mountain in Arizona where Jesus met with me. It was a powerful moment in my life. That moment kept me going. It was not, though, the moment when I realized God was for real about redeeming my most broken places. That was not the moment I claimed it. That happened a year later.

One year later to the day. Three hundred and sixty-five days of moving forward.

Daniel died on February 23, 2003. That night I didn't sleep. I stayed up all night in overwhelming sadness and punishing grief. One year later, February 23, 2004, I stayed up all night again, this time for a different reason. In fact, I was so focused on that reason that I had no conscious remembrance that it was the one-year anniversary of Daniel's death. That had been the date of my darkest moment, but I didn't even remember it because February 23, 2004, was when my first daughter, Mary, was born after a long night up with my wife, Rachel, in a hospital room. On February 23. I held Mary and cried again.

It was some days later that I realized the day of my greatest grief was now also the day of my greatest joy. I remember checking the calendar. (They were paper back then.) I turned the pages of the previous year's calendar to find out if it could be so. I hadn't marked the day of Daniel's death in my heart. I had tried to forget it. But there it was in my spiral-bound planner as clear as day. February 23.

That moment, I chose hope. I was actually holding hope in my arms. I was still a full-time student. I would go to school, then to work, and then come home to finally hold Mary. Rachel would go to bed, and I would stay up on the couch holding Mary and watching March Madness. So many nights I would stare at her little face and know that I couldn't close off my heart. Even though life was hard and I was tired, I had to stay open. I had to heal. I had to keep going.

It wasn't like Mary's life replaced the life of Daniel. Of course not; that could never happen. Her birth didn't even replace the sadness—I still carry sadness over the loss of Daniel. But I couldn't overlook the fact that it was the same exact day. It was a redemptive moment for me, a moment when God saved something. God saved me. It gave me something that I almost lost: hope. And I claimed it. I grabbed it.

I want to ask you to believe in a redemptive moment that is coming for you. You can't even see it yet. I am not asking you to believe it when you see it. I am asking you to believe it *until* you see it.

We all have breaking points, breaking moments. Would you choose to break open? To let go? Try opening your hands up right now. As you physically open your hands, think about the things you need to let go of in your heart. Breathe out what you need to let go of to keep going. Breathe in the resolve to keep moving.

To choose hope.

To let go is to choose hope. To keep going when your body and mind say that you can't go on is to choose hope.

To choose hope is the opposite of losing hope. And we all lose hope sometimes. For now let's just believe together that there is hope. We can let go, we can keep going, because we have reason to hope. Believe that God has a full, good life coming for you. Let hope fill you deep in your being.

Maybe you aren't there yet. I get it, and it's okay. I'm going to believe it for you as we continue on.

two

SPACE, NOT PACE

We must not forget that it is not a thing that
lends significance to a moment; it is the
moment that lends significance to things.

ABRAHAM HESCHEL

I sit with people who are dying.

On a regular basis I sit by the bedside of someone who knows that they have only days or hours to live. As a pastor I am invited to join people who are breathing their last breaths. There are a few professions in which people get to do this, and I have one of them. I say "get to do this" because it is a great gift.

You might be surprised to know that when people are dying, they don't spend all that much time thinking or talking about dying. Sure, they commonly mention feeling afraid or uncertain. At times there are questions about death or what happens after you die. A pastor or chaplain is usually called in to discuss such things. But I would say the primary tone and content of discussion is not what we might expect.

People who are dying talk about living. They talk about life.

They share stories about their lives. They focus on moments when they really experienced life. They recount memories of family members that lead to smiles across faces, bellies shaking with laughter, and even singing. It's true.

Paula was the first person I sat with before she died. She hadn't spoken or responded to us in a few days. I remember standing by Paula's bedside when, after days of not a word spoken, she began to sing with us the words of a song she knew by heart. "He walks with me, and talks with me, and tells me I am his own."[1]

When people are dying, their hearts remember life. Because their hearts are alive. Rarely do folks who are dying talk about promotions at work, how much money they made, or awards won.

These are things we spend a lot of time pining for, but they aren't what is remembered, what is cherished. Instead, people talk about Christmas morning when they found their children had woken in the night and unwrapped presents without the parents. They talk about jumping off the dock at the lake, ice cream at the Braves game when it must have been 100 degrees, and the time Dad came out of the ocean wave that knocked him down and left his swimming suit somewhere in the Pacific.

I'll be honest. They never talk about money. Never talk about business. Never talk about crushing it from age forty to fifty-five to move from middle management to senior leadership at the firm. It's not to say those things aren't important and don't set people and future family members up for success. I'm just saying it's not what will be on our minds and on the tip of our tongues when we have two hours to go. People talk about the drive home after leaving their son at college for the first time. They talk about Thanksgiving when Grandpa prayed his short and simple prayer of blessing, when Uncle Frank farted during church, or when their daughter sang her first solo in the school choir. They talk about the picnic blanket, lying on their back, holding hands, watching the sun move through the clouds. They talk about life.

Those moments are the ones you will talk about when your life here is ending and you are looking to the next. I think it is actually a common thread that holds us in this life and then goes with us to the next. The life stories shared before death all include one common thing: space. Not like space, the final frontier. No, just simply space in your life to breathe. The end-of-life memories that are lifted up are the ones when intentional space was set aside, or found by surprise, where people could actually live and breathe and love and laugh.

One common denominator for real-life moments is the *space* for life to happen.

You need space.

And if breaking open is the way we are talking about moving through the hard and broken places of life, you will have to find and make space for that to happen.

THE LIFELESS LIFE

In the mornings when I wake up, I try to look at my phone plugged in on my bedside table, but the cord that charges it is not quite long enough. So I have to lean out of my bed and grab the phone to keep it plugged in. It's a sort of contortionist act as I hang my torso off the bed while keeping my legs on the mattress for balance. This is my only core exercise for the day. I would get a new cord, but the only time I ever think about it being too short is in this moment between sleep and waking, when I'm hoping I'll get to sleep longer.

Yet, somehow, almost every morning when I look at the time, I have one minute before my alarm goes off. I love the rare days when I look at the time and realize that I have three more hours to go. But lately I am waking up with just a one-minute cushion between me and moving from horizontal to vertical. One minute before right on time. And by "right on time," I mean the time I decided the night before would be the closest that I could cut it to get going to get it all done. Before I go to bed, I do this reverse timing technique from the moment I have to be in my car backward through coffee, kids' lunches being made, feeding the dogs, my back stretches (bulging disk, y'all!), shower, and prayer, to feet hitting the floor. It is some *Beautiful Mind* kind of math. (Shout-out to Mrs. Sharpe's eleventh-grade algebra class!)

I can't tell you how many vacation cups of coffee I have had while vowing to do better at this. It would be hard to count how many journal pages I have written about getting a new routine, becoming more disciplined in my schedule, and doing better to incorporate my hobbies and passions. But for quite some time I have been zooming through my mornings only to zoom through my day, to hopefully catch the end of the Braves game at night, to setting my reverse-timing alarm clock for the next morning. Cramped. Tired. Fast. Hanging off the bed hoping it's 2:30 a.m., not 5:30 a.m. No wonder my back hurts.

If you have a cramped life, then I get your cramped life. Most of us would say, "That's life."

But then there are those times when something different happens. When life bursts through.

My oldest daughter, Mary, is seventeen now. That's right—the one I told you whose birth brought me back to life is now about to be living on her own. We are taking college visits. (Excuse me. I need to do some deep breathing exercises for a moment . . .

Okay. I'm back.)

We are taking college visits. I drive her to a college on her list and an upperclassman student, usually a boy who has not combed his hair this semester, walks us around for a campus tour. But on our last college visit something different happened. We were driving four hours north to a university in Kentucky. We got up early, stopped at Starbucks on the way out, and as soon as we hit the interstate, I noticed this different thing. Mary was not looking at her phone. Had she forgotten it? Was the battery dead? Was she in handcuffs? No, no, and no. She was just sitting there, sipping her drink, looking out the window and talking to me. I played it cool and pretended not to notice that I was living in an alternate universe, but my heart was swelling. We didn't discuss anything of great importance, but it was the discussion itself that was of great importance. We talked for hours. Hours.

Then, she took a nap. I looked over at her profile and, as any parent can, saw the profile that I memorized when I held her as a newborn baby. This is something God allows us to see so we can feel what his heart feels like. And so we don't abandon our children in the wild.

After a while Mary woke up and we drove through the small

downtown of the liberal arts university town. We had a hot dog at a little café on the corner of Main Street. Mary got hot-dog juice on her new jeans that purposefully have holes in them. We did some cleanup work, but it was a solid grease stain. (The stain is still there. Turns out the new jeans were her sister's. That is a story for another day. Too soon.)

We took our campus visit with a tousled-haired boy who wore khakis he must have slept in. Mary held her new university-branded folder over her hot-dog stain as we walked. We were paired with a family who clearly asked more annoying questions than we did. Mary was able to tour the athletics facility with some other cheerleaders who were recruiting her to their team. I kept my distance and we reconvened at my truck. I could tell it was a good visit.

We began our four-hour drive home and stopped for a burger after a while. We talked about the colleges we had visited in the last few weeks, and I could feel my heart being stretched almost to breaking thinking about her living in a different city. I tried to ask her more questions than give advice. It was something I had been struggling to do. She still hadn't touched the phone. My heart leaped. *She still had not touched the phone!*

Then she asked if I wanted to listen to Taylor Swift. "Uh, yeah." And we listened to an entire album. Mary had a Taylor Swift birthday party when she was seven. We know every word to the thirteen-song album *Fearless*, and we sang them all loudly in my Tacoma just like Taylor would have wanted us to do. Then we turned to an album I used to listen to with my dad, Paul Simon's *Graceland*, and kept it loud all the way back to Nashville.

As we pulled back onto the little country road we live on, just moments from home, Mary said, "Dad, this was really a great day."

I gulped. "Yes, it was, Mary."

I have a feeling. I mean, there is a chance . . . it's possible she and I might talk about that day if I am fortunate enough to have her standing nearby when I have two hours left.

And it wasn't just Mary who made space that day.

I think about what leads to a day like that because I want to have more days like it. And I know what it is. Space. When the alarm went off that morning, I had one thing on the calendar. Mary. That leaves a lot of other space.

There was some breaking that day. You break a bit when you see your oldest daughter walking around a college campus, laughing at bad rehearsed jokes from a twenty-one-year-old accounting-major tour guide. You break a bit when you begin to picture her living four hours away from home. This is a necessary breaking, and, if ventured in the right way, it can lead to life for both dad and daughter. But it doesn't happen without the space.

We all have things to do. Many of us have to clock in and clock out at work. We have obligations to fulfill. That is actually life too. All of life is not singing Taylor Swift at the top of your lungs with the windows down. (That's what heaven is like.) You get it. Life, by nature, includes the mundane and the routine. But that doesn't mean our destiny is cramped lives with no space for the good stuff. *We need space.*

INTO A WIDER SPACE

There are three steps to finding space to live:

- First, notice the ache.

- Next, interrupt the pace.

- Then, intentionally create space.

Notice the ache.

First, we have to notice that we are hurting. We might have to pause for a moment here, because there are all kinds of ways the ache can be numbed. Some of us are experts at ignoring the ache. We may have an unintentional routine to push it down every day. This can look like four glasses instead of one on Tuesday night. Or four episodes of *The Crown* on a sunny Saturday. This can look like hitting ignore on the iPhone when your best friend is calling on the drive home from work. *Why did I hit ignore? I hit ignore because I don't want to go there.* But the most common technique for numbing the ache is to keep adding things to do and to keep moving at light speed. If you keep doing and keep moving, you have a chance at making it through a day or a hundred days and not even noticing the ache.

Most of us have found a way to sit on top of the ache. It's there. We know it, but as long as we can stay on top of it, we won't have to pay attention to it, much less feel it.

I believe that noticing the ache will be the best thing you can do in this season of your life. It has the potential to be the first step toward hope, healing, and wholeness in your life.

How do you notice the ache? The best way I have found is to be aware of when I can't or won't or don't want to do things that are truly life. I'm not talking about being depressed here, though those are certainly signs I might feel depressed. I think a lot of us may not consider ourselves depressed but can relate to having less energy and initiative toward the people and the things we love. This is a strange paradox. It is a strange way to live when the things you would say are the most important to you are actually the things you give less and less of your time to.

Jesus said, "Where your treasure is, there your heart will be also" (Matthew 6:21). Upon first reading that, we nod our heads and get that Jesus was saying there is a connection between our treasure and our hearts. There is a connection between, say, our money and our hearts. There is a connection between where we are investing our time and energy and our hearts. But we usually take this to mean that our treasure will follow our hearts. We value our family, friends, church, passions. They are our hearts, and so we will find our treasure there too. But that is not what Jesus was saying.

He was not saying your treasure follows your heart. He was saying your heart will follow your treasure. Where you are investing your time, energy, and money will become your treasure. That's why a lot of us have things that we say are our treasure, but they aren't really our treasure anymore. We gave so much time, energy, and money to other places that our hearts followed. We obligated and scheduled ourselves to the point that there is no room, no space, for the things we truly value. And that numbs us; it's the unintended consequence of giving our lives to things we don't value.

Who would say they value wine? (Okay, I see your hand up. But hang with me.) Who would say they value the excess of wine or binge-watching a show? These are not our treasures, but we give a lot of time, energy, and money to these things, and it creates a gap between our hearts and our true treasures. Thus the numb feeling, and thus the ache. But we sit on top of the ache and try to keep doing enough so we don't notice it.

So how do we notice it? We take a moment (like this moment) to see if there are places in our lives where there might be a gap between what we say is most important and what we are actually giving our lives to. We notice if we can't or won't or don't want to do things that are truly life to us. That is a sign of numbness and a sign that we are sitting on top of the ache.

My moment was at age thirty-six, sitting on the front porch with a six-year-old Phoebe standing next to me. Phoebe is my youngest. Phoebe loves dinosaurs, alpacas, and riding scooters (in that order, according to her). She is imaginative and spunky and basically the most fun person you will ever be around. I was sitting on the front porch and Phoebe asked me, "Dad, do you want to play?"

I said no. I never looked at her. In fact, I never took my gaze off the trees in the front yard. I never saw her expression when I said no. I'm not sure which way she went when she walked away. But I did feel something. That's why I can write about it today. I felt an ache.

It came a few moments later, but for a moment I went from on top of the ache to just barely dipping my toe in it. I pondered that moment, when I told my treasure that I had no time or energy for her.

Now, sometimes you can't or even don't want to play with your kids. That is called *normal*. What I was experiencing was also normal, but normal for the person who has no space to live. I noticed that I had said no to my treasure when I had no reason to say no. When my days are numbered, I know I will long for more moments playing dinosaurs with Phoebe in the front yard.

So what was the no? It was evidence of the ache—and I noticed it. That moment was the potential for the best kind of breaking. But I had a long way to go. I had patterns and habits that would have to be undone. I had time, energy, and money flowing in directions that had to change. And I noticed it.

With no space you will unknowingly sit on top of the ache, and that is a dangerous place to live. It's what leads to the mistakes that destroy lives, because we are so numb it takes something really dangerous to feel again.

Interrupt the pace.

After we notice the ache, we interrupt the pace. For most of us that means slowing down, even stopping. If our pace is too fast, interrupting means we will need to step on the brakes. But for some of us it may mean we need to get moving. If we have stopped all operations and are way down in the numbing, we might have to step it up. The point is we must jar the current pace enough that it will get the heart's attention.

It may be hard to believe, but we can dictate the pace of our lives. We have the right to set boundaries. (Someone should write a book about that.)[2] To do this, we will have to pay attention to our yeses and our nos. What we say yes to and what we say no to will have to change to interrupt the pace. For a season you may have to say no to some regular yeses. This will interrupt the pace. It will get the heart's attention and, like I said, for most of us it will stop us a bit.

And it's here that we can go to step three, to intentionally create space. I know I was brief in discussing step two, but if we notice the ache, that will be the pace interrupter we need. The ache will make us aware and even compel us to interrupt the pace. In other words, we will have no choice but to pay attention and stop, and in that place we can do the thing that will change us forever. That will give us moments that will stay in our memories. It will actually give life.

Intentionally create space.

I am using the word *intentionally* here because I have learned that this will just not happen. It requires intentionality. Wide, open spaces do not just appear, though it feels that way sometimes. Someone might say, "I was out on this hike, and two hours in, I walked into a wide-open field. The flowers were blooming. The birds were singing. And there I met with God." Or I will hear, "I had my cup of coffee, the Bible was open, everything was still, and God spoke to me through the reading that day." It seems as if the "space" appears out of nowhere, but actually the space for the space was created. The hike, the hours, the early morning coffee, the open Bible—they were all intentional acts that created space.

Each one of us has to figure out what that space looks like for us. I won't presume to know what you need at this time, what the space looks like for you. For me, at age thirty-six, it looked like going to counseling. Now, I have said no to playing with my kids a thousand times in my run as a dad. What I noticed that time was different. I noticed an ache below the surface. And I could tell if I did another twenty years at my same pace, then I would be a fifty-six-year-old who was numb to the voices and touches of the people I treasure. I have met such fifty-six-year-olds. That's not who I want to be. It was a drastic moment for me—a dramatic noticing that led me to want to interrupt my pace once a week with a thirty-minute drive to a counselor and an hour on the couch talking about it. That inter-ruption of pace helped me intentionally create space where, though there are still some times I am too tired or busy to play, I'm moving at a pace where I can say yes way more often to a make-believe front-yard game where I am an alpaca being chased by a T-Rex. And that makes me feel very, very alive.

For Nicodemus, in the Bible, it looked like canceling a meeting one night and going to talk to someone after work. What became the most famous sentence in the Bible started with one guy who, I think, noticed the ache, interrupted the pace, and created some space. A simple change of pace led to his life being saved. And it led to a line that has brought so many people to belief that they might have life in Jesus and life forever. The line is "For God so loved the world that he gave his one and only Son, that whoever believes in him shall not perish but have eternal life." That is John 3:16, the most famous verse in the Bible. And for good reason. It holds it all. But the line was written to conclude a story about Nicodemus visiting Jesus.

Nicodemus was a religious teacher and leader. He was a part of the group that was supposed to have it all together—the very group that would eventually campaign for Jesus' conviction and cruci-fixion. But Nicodemus was seeking something more. That's one of the things I love about Nicodemus. He was clearly a member and clearly a seeker. He was a member of the religious group, and yet he still had some stuff he was working through, and he sought Jesus to help answer those questions.

"He came to Jesus at night and said, 'Rabbi, we know that you are a teacher who has come from God. For no one could perform the signs you are doing if God were not with him'" (John 3:2).

Nicodemus came to Jesus at night. I'll stop there. Coming to Jesus at night is clearly Nicodemus interrupting his pace and creating some different space to encounter Jesus and ask questions of him. I don't know Nicodemus's regular routine, but I assure you it wasn't his custom to have clandestine meetings with renegade rabbis. Nicodemus was supposed to have all the answers. He had been to all the schools. But he was asking Jesus about God.

It's only because I can relate to Nicodemus so much that I make the presumption—which I don't think is too far of a stretch—that Nicodemus was at a breaking point. I think he was noticing an ache.

Because I am a religious teacher, because I can relate to Nicodemus, I think that he was in the midst of a crisis. Religion wasn't working for him. He had given his life to it; he was a member of the club. But he needed something new. He needed a breakthrough. I think it's possible that Nicodemus was facing a breakdown—and, yes, it's possible to be in church each week and still feel broken down.

The thing Jesus said Nicodemus needed was a new birth. A new start. A whole new life.

Jesus replied, "Very truly I tell you, no one can see the kingdom of God unless they are born again" (John 3:3).

Jesus knew Nicodemus's heart and he said he needed a new birth. Not a new teaching, not a refresher course on the things of God. Jesus said he needed to be born again.

Nicodemus asked, "How can someone be born when they are old?" (v. 4).

That may be what you are thinking too. *How can I do that? I'm forty!*

Or maybe you are caught up on other earthly reasons you can't be born again. You have too many miles under your belt, too much built up, too much baggage to have that kind of change.

Jesus began to explain to Nicodemus that what he was talking about was not bound by physical limitations. He wasn't talking about a physical rebirth but a spiritual one; and the things of the Spirit are not bound by the same limitations of the physical.

Nicodemus said, "You want me to go back in my mother's womb?"

And Jesus was like, "For real? No, I don't want you to go back in your mother's womb, you weirdo."

His actual words were "Flesh gives birth to flesh, but the Spirit gives birth to spirit" (v. 6).

Jesus was inviting Nicodemus to let his spirit come alive again. For the dying, dead parts to be birthed again. And I don't want to get graphic or weird like Nicodemus, but the birth that Jesus wants to give us is as dramatic a breaking open as our physical birth. Our physical birth involved crying and pain and water and blood, and our new birth in the Spirit will involve crying and pain and water and blood.

We will get there, but remember, for Nicodemus to begin his journey toward life he had to go visit Jesus at night. Nicodemus had to find some space to encounter and hear from Jesus.

The first step in breaking open is creating space. When we embark on a new journey, we usually think of increasing the pace, but Jesus' way is creating space.

Nicodemus had to cancel a meeting or skip a couple of episodes of *The Great British Baking Show* (don't judge). He had to make some space to get before Jesus.

That is the invitation for us in this moment. Ask, *Where do I need to create space so I can encounter Jesus?*

The question is worth considering. Because either way, breaking is on the horizon. If we don't notice the ache, there is still a breaking. Aches that are ignored lead to paces that are increased, which lead to cramped lifestyles that have one common ending: good old-fashioned breakdown.

So for now,

- notice,

- interrupt,

- create.

Seek to do something that is outside of your normal routine. Notice the ache, interrupt the pace, create some space. That's all Nicodemus did. I find it so fascinating that John (the guy who wrote the book of John in the Bible) summed up Nicodemus's (an old religious leader who was still seeking) encounter with Jesus by saying, *God loves the world so much that he sent his Son so we could live.* Instead of breaking down, Nicodemus broke open as evidenced by the rest of his story—but that's something we will look at later.

THE GIFT OF SPACE

For now, I think God is trying to show us that *we have permission to do this.* We have permission to stop. It is in this space that we find hope, healing, and wholeness for life. Throughout the story of God's people, we find folks who got so distracted that they forgot

God. Then they started doing all kinds of things to try to get well and find life, and nothing worked. The only thing that worked was God sending his Son into the world. For them and for us, that's where life is found.

Jesus is encountered in the space that is created by stopping—and I don't just mean vacation. If we stop only on vacation, we will have miserable vacations as our bodies try to adjust to abruptly stopping. We have permission to stop *today*.

Here's why this noticing, interrupting, and creating margin is so important.

It frees us up for

- space to grieve,

- space to give thanks,

- space to breathe,

- space to think,

- and space to delight.

Space to Grieve

This is where we start. So many of us need to grieve. I'll find myself crying sometimes reading something in *Sports Illustrated* and realize, *Oh. I need to grieve something.* (I mean, when you read about a four-year manager on the high school basketball team getting to play in the final moments of his senior year and hitting a three-point basket, you can shed a couple of tears. But weeping may point to something else.) So much of what is expressing itself in our lives is grief, but we've provided no space to grieve. The divorce. Mom's death. The miscarriage. They lead to great grief. I get it; these losses happen and we still have to go back to work. But noticing and interrupting the pace for a season can lead you to create some beautiful space to grieve. And we all need that space. I encounter a lot of adults who are complaining about all manner of things in their lives that don't matter one bit, and it's because they haven't grieved their losses.

Space to Give Thanks

It's really easy to get worn down by the things in life that aren't going the way we hoped. We can count those things up and make a list easily. Often, if we examine our conversations, we find we're actually spending many minutes, if not hours, in the day listing the gaps between what we expected life to be like and what it is really like. Those gaps are a reality and should be noticed and noted. But those things come out easily. What doesn't come as naturally is gratitude. That's why I suggest that you create space to give thanks.

I do a thing I call "gratitude Saturday." I start my Saturday with a cup of coffee as I sit by a window in my house, and I simply list the things I am grateful for. There are many common themes that arise each week, and common people, but what I find is that every week I have new and beautiful things that I am thankful for. That Saturday space has become a time that I long for. I wonder, *What new thing do I have to be thankful for this week?* And I find that I end up sharing about those things throughout the day and the following week. That simple space I created in the morning spills into other spaces.

Space to Breathe

There was a season when I would let out sighs that didn't sound like sighs. Typically a sigh is just a simple exhalation of air. It's not that loud or that noticeable—or so I thought. Well, I was sighing, and it sounded like a Lamaze childbirth class. Rachel would ask me in the car, "Did you hear that?" I wouldn't have even noticed what was happening. But it was a physiological function of my body trying to get air out. It was the result of many, many short breaths over the course of the day, in which I literally was not getting enough oxygen in and carbon dioxide out. So my body was reacting and getting it all out. It was also, of course, using this physiological function to show me something that was going on emotionally and mentally. Believe it or not, the space we are talking about creating will actually give you space to breathe. It's about life. And breath is life.

Space to Think

Many of us are simply not thinking well right now. We aren't thinking enough for ourselves. We fill up our downtime with the phone or a news station, and instead of thinking, we just receive information.

We are only taking in outside information, data, and opinions. This, of course, leads us to reacting rather than responding. The people of God need to think. And you have to have space to do that.

I know someone who does his best thinking in the woods. He is a very busy business owner and leader, but he takes time every day for a walk or jog in the woods because that is the space where he can think. It slows his mind down. He is moving, but moving at a different pace—and it's there that he has space.

Space to Delight

Grieving. Thanking. Breathing. Thinking.

Living.

God loves us so much that he sent Jesus so we could live.

God loves us so much. God loves you so much. So much.

We need space to take that in. *Space to delight and be delighted in.* God loves you and wants to delight in you.

There is a connection between space and delight.

I love to be delighted in. Most of us do, even if it has been awhile since that has happened. I love hearing, "Daddy's home!" I love getting a big bro-hug (most of the time). I love when Rachel laughs at me and with me and delights in me. Sometimes I go a whole week without stopping to delight in the people I love. If we say we don't delight much, my guess is we don't have much space.

David said in Psalm 18:19, "He brought me out into a spacious place; he rescued me because he delighted in me." God put him in a spacious place and rescued him. God loved him so much that he gave him life. Why? To delight in him.

Breaking open leads to the space where we learn that God delights in us. And God delights in *us*, not in what we do. A parent can like what their kids do, but more importantly they really just delight in their kids, not in what they are up to. My daughter Lydia raised a pig this year. (*How many daughters does this dude have?* you might be wondering. Three. The answer is three.) Lydia raised a pig in the Future Farmers of America club. In the FFA they call it a hog. I learned they are the same thing. They said her hog was a little hog. It weighed 280 pounds. Lydia spent months raising this hog from a hogling . . . hoglet . . . I'm not sure what you call a baby hog . . . to this big ol' 280-pound hog. And then there was a hog show. I took two days off work and spent it in a hog barn with hundreds of hogs. And Lydia. I don't always delight in what my kids do, but I do delight in my kids.

You know what I loved? The space with Lydia.

In the garden in the very beginning, God walked with Adam and Eve in the cool of the day (Genesis 3:8). God spent time with them. God sent Jesus to give us eternal life to get us back to the garden where there is unending life and the presence of God. But in this life now, through intentionally created space, God gets us back to that space where we delight, and he delights in us. This can happen in really busy lives. Some of the busiest families I know are the ones who have this down. They know to pay attention to how everyone is feeling, interrupt the pace from time to time, and stop in created spaces to delight. It's a beautiful mess, but we can get there.

So remember our steps:

1. Notice the ache.

2. Interrupt the pace.

3. Intentionally create space.

Why would we do this hard work?

To have space where

- we grieve and heal,

- we give thanks and gain perspective,

- we breathe and catch our breath,

- we think and process for ourselves,

- we delight and are delighted in.

Life.

That sounds worth it.

Let's do a few things right now.

Notice one way you are sitting on top of the ache right now. Ask, *How am I numbing and ignoring so as to avoid the ache?*

Notice it.

Life.

Think of one place in your life where you can interrupt the pace. Ask, *What is a different pace, and where can I take it?*

Interrupt it.

Life.

Seek to create one space this week to intentionally stop. Ask, *Do I need space to grieve, thank, breathe, think, or delight?*

Intentionally create it.

Life.

The counselor I went to see after I noticed the ache asked me to consider interrupting my normal cycle of overworking and under-processing. He encouraged me to take some steps out of the routine that had left me so numb. Rachel and I decided that rather than our normal, annual vacation to the beach, we would go to a remote lake in the mountains. We sought to do something different. Something that would be less work for us. When you have young kids, taking them to the beach is the equivalent of preparing an army for battle every day. Upon arriving at the lake, we weren't so sure. There were very few distractions and very few activities that we didn't have to create. (There were no go-cart tracks nearby. There was literally no Putt-Putt!) The girls were a bit leery as well, and the uncertain Wi-Fi made this situation even more precarious. But we figured it out. We learned how to catch bluegill in the lake, some of them measuring over three inches long! We put together a puzzle or two. We read books in a hammock. We breathed.

And on a June night we heard from the local news that a "strawberry moon" would be right over the lake at 11:00 p.m. and that we shouldn't miss it. There wouldn't be a cloud in the sky. I didn't know what the strawberry moon was, but you know I googled it! I learned it is the last full moon of spring and gets its name from the time when strawberries are harvested. The girls and I planned a late-night swim in the lake. We invited Mama, but she said no way. Mom was not into being up late that night or jumping in freezing, mountain stream-fed lake water. The girls and I were not deterred. We waited until the news station had said the moon would be brightest and biggest, and we walked to the dock. Someone made the mistake of dipping a toe in the water. That created a fifteen-minute discussion about the effects of hypothermia. Finally, the decision was made to jump in at the same time.

"One . . . two . . . Are you sure?"

"Okay, yes, yes, we are doing this."

"One . . . two . . . three!"

Holding hands, we jumped off the dock together. Seven minutes later I began to regain feeling in my legs. We splashed around with only the light of the moon illuminating the water and our faces as we laughed and hollered out. We watched the ripples of the water in the moonlight and eventually relaxed to the point of floating in life jackets in silence under the strawberry moon. Then, we heard a scream and another splash. Mom had joined us. Mom was shrieking. We weren't sure she was okay. But we were all cracking up. It is rumored that Mom came down in her bathrobe to check on us and then spontaneously made the decision to jump in. I can neither confirm nor deny what she was wearing or not wearing that night. But I know it made a big impression on us. I know I started crying real tears of joy writing this for you just now. I know we still talk about it today and probably will talk about it in a holy family circle around a bed someday. And I know we had come to that lake barely breathing. We had come breaking in so many ways. And I know, in that space we created, there is no doubt—we were fully alive.

three

RISING UP, NOT HUNKERING DOWN

We will be able to hew out of the mountain
of despair a stone of hope.

MARTIN LUTHER KING JR.

Threshing wheat in a winepress.

That's what Gideon was doing when he had reached his lowest point. Threshing wheat in a winepress.

Sometimes because of life circumstances outside our control, and a little bit of brokenness, we will start doing something that makes no sense. And then we do the thing that makes no sense so long that the things that make sense *don't* make sense—because we have been doing the thing that makes no sense so long that it seems normal. Make sense?

For Gideon the "thing that made no sense" was threshing wheat in a winepress. His story is found in the book of Judges in the Bible. When you hear people talk about him, it's usually only about how he laid out the fleeces to test if God's declarations were for real. Gideon became known as a hero, a mighty warrior, in a time when there wasn't much good to talk about. But before all that he was threshing wheat in a winepress.

Most of us probably know little about the ancient techniques for making bread and wine. But we wouldn't be surprised to know that wheat had to be threshed and grapes had to be pressed. And, even with our limited knowledge of three-thousand-year-old Middle Eastern agricultural practices, we can easily surmise that wheat was not supposed to be threshed where grapes were pressed. A winepress is for making wine. And a threshing floor is where the process of separating wheat happens.

Gideon was threshing the wheat in the winepress.

Why?

He was hiding out. He was lying low. He was hunkering down. Gideon lived in a time when his people, the Israelites, were an oppressed people. They were under a seven-year oppression by the Midianites. Not only that, but the people of God had taken on the idols and begun to worship the gods of the other people groups in the new land. They forgot God, forgot his ways, forgot his commands.

Gideon's people, the Israelites, were the ones who'd been slaves in Egypt. God rescued them and took them across the Red Sea. God provided bread for them on the ground every day in the wilderness. He gave them his cloud in the sky to follow by day and his fire in the sky to stop them at night. All the while, they were looking forward to the promise of the promised land. This was the place God had prepared for them to live and thrive. It was a land flowing with milk and honey. It was everything they needed and everything they dreamed of. And when they got there, the people of God forgot about God.

In Gideon's time they were living in the promised land, but they were seven years into living under the harsh hand of another people.

Midian was so oppressive that Gideon's people lived in mountain clefts and caves. The Israelites, once slaves, were slaves again. Hunkered down in the mountains, hiding.

Whenever the Israelites attempted to plant crops, the Midianites would invade and steal from them. They took their sheep, their cattle—their donkeys, for crying out loud. They took everything. They even took their wheat.

God's promised land, which would have provided for the Israelites and their families for generations, was pillaged by Midianite marauders.

And then something happened.

The Israelites remembered something.

They remembered someone.

They remembered God.

"Midian so impoverished the Israelites that they cried out to the Lord for help" (Judges 6:6).

This didn't happen easily. They had to become "so impoverished," so worn out, so broken that they remembered God. And God sent an angel, who came and sat down under a notable oak tree—the oak tree of Joash. Sometimes a God story gets weirder before it gets better. Or it gets weirder as it gets better. The same will be true for our lives.

Listen to how Scripture says it: "The angel of the LORD came and sat down under the oak in Ophrah that belonged to Joash the Abiezrite, where his son Gideon was threshing wheat in a winepress to keep it from the Midianites. When the angel of the LORD appeared to Gideon, he said, 'The LORD is with you, mighty warrior'" (Judges 6:11–12).

Gideon was trying to make bread. Bread was everything to the people of God. Bread was good. It was life. *Preach!* Eating bread was what you did when life was good—when you were with the family, with your people, around the table, remembering God, eating bread.

This process of making bread began on the threshing floor; that's where threshing wheat was supposed to take place. A threshing floor was a flat place, a spacious place that had been cleared. The clearing was important because of what took place in the threshing. Threshing is the process by which grain is broken apart. It is broken into kernels, chaff (the husks that held the kernels), and straw (the stalks on which the grain grows).

Threshing is the breaking part. On a threshing floor the wheat is beaten and crushed. If you are fortunate, you have large animals to pull something over the threshing floor to break it up. But if the Midianites had stolen all your livestock, threshing would involve picking up the pieces of wheat, throwing them in the air, and allowing them to separate. The kernels fall and the chaff blows away. It'd be messy. But a wide-open threshing floor would make it bearable.

Gideon could not afford the risk of standing in a wide-open space, but the wheat-breaking was necessary. Thus, Gideon was threshing wheat down in a hole—in a winepress, to be specific.

What's a winepress? It's a place to smash grapes, and it's usually found in a hole in the ground. In Gideon's day winepresses were caves of rock, good for smashing grapes. So Gideon was in a hole in the ground made for smashing grapes and using his bare hands to thresh wheat.[1] He threw wheat into the air, but it didn't blow away like it would on a threshing floor. It fell into his eyes, his mouth, his lungs. Threshing wheat was hard enough; threshing wheat in a winepress was miserable. It is the picture of frustration and oppression. You cower, you cough, you curse.

Like threshing wheat, breaking open is hard enough when you have space. If you are hunkered down in a hole, it's miserable. And that's where some of us are right now. As we consider breaking open to life, we are hunkered down. We fear real and obvious enemies. We are embarrassed, and we are defeated. Some of us are doing something that once was an obvious sign of our brokenness, and now that we've been doing it so long, it feels, well, just normal.

So hear this.

God found Gideon right there in the hole in the ground. And called him out.

His angel came and sat down under Gideon's dad's tree and said, "The LORD is with you, mighty warrior" (v. 12).

This statement was ironic, preposterous, even foolish to Gideon's ears. A mighty warrior? Hiding in a hole?

Gideon responded as politely as he could. "Pardon me, my lord"

(v. 13). In other words, "You have the wrong guy." Gideon reminded God's angel that he was from the weakest family from the weakest tribe. His low estate and his family's ineptitude were right on the tip of his tongue. "Me? A mighty warrior? I'm in a hole choking on wheat while I fear my enemies."

Okay, that was a lot.

But we can feel the connection to our lives. Threshing wheat in a winepress is a substitute for the real thing. When we settle for bread made in winepresses, we are nowhere near the good life that God holds for us. What a mess. How do we get out? What do we do when the enemies are real? And how do we even notice when we have grown so used to our holes?

SETTLING FOR AN IMITATION

I took my daughters to the World of Coca-Cola museum in Atlanta, Georgia. Didn't see that coming, did you? Yeah, I did! Do you know about this magical place? The World of Coca-Cola museum shares the story of Coca-Cola. It exhibits Coca-Cola artifacts. You can get your picture made with the polar bear, and the elusive and secret Coke recipe is kept in a vault there. And perhaps best of all, you get all the Coke you can drink.

The first taste of Coke on the museum tour comes after you have waited in a long, winding line that starts outside, goes up some steps, and then to closed doors that are opened by real-life human Coca-Cola greeters with name tags that tell what country they are from. The first room you enter is an air-conditioned lobby with a big, long bar that serves drinks—I'm talking dark brown carbonated goodness. All the Cokes you can drink. It's all free, if you forget you paid $34.95 apiece to walk in the place. And I did! I forgot! I just felt like I was being offered the grace of as many cans of Coke as I wanted.

I walked up to the bar with my girls and grabbed a green can of Coke. I looked at it and saw it was called Coca-Cola Life. Really attractive can. I liked the way it looked. Green means good now—healthy. *It must be good for the environment*, I assumed. I opened it up. I was in the World of Coke with people from all around the world, sipping this ice-cold drink, and it was really good.

I realized in that moment that Coca-Cola Life was one of the newer versions of Coke. They come out all the time. I still remember New Coke when I was kid. (What's up, 1980s?!) There is of course Diet Coke, Caffeine-Free Coke, Coke Zero. Well, Coca-Cola Life has 35 percent fewer calories than normal Coke and uses cane sugar and stevia, whatever that is.[2] I drank it and I thought, *This is good. Pretty dang good.*

Then I looked down and saw my girls were all drinking the red can. Coca-Cola Classic. And as I drank out of the green can, I kept noticing their red cans. Me, green can. Them, red can. I stopped drinking. I asked one of them for a sip of theirs. (Sip-of-yours is my favorite drink anyway.) I wanted to see if I could taste the difference. Like, how much different could it be?

Could the color of the can and the source of the sweetness really make that much difference? The moment I put the red can in my hand, I could feel the difference. My senses seemed to wake up as I lifted it to my mouth, and when it hit my lips, I felt the need to repent. I felt like I should confess in a loud voice, to all who could hear me, the error of my ways. "I don't know why I grabbed the green can! It looked good. It said 'Life' on it, but it led to death (of my tastebuds at least). I'm so, so sorry. There is one Coke and his name is Classic!"

I threw away my Coca-Cola Life and went and got what we called when I was a kid *the real thing*.

I'm sure Gideon and his family were eating bread from that winepress. And it was bread, so it was good. But I wonder at what point they forgot what real good bread made from wheat from the threshing floor tasted like. Did they forget what bread tasted like when it was made in the spacious place, when their eyes weren't dimmed and their backs weren't stooped and their lungs were clear? They were so hunkered down, so laid low, that I wonder if they even remembered there was a real thing that was better.

Through his angel, God told Gideon, "The LORD is with you, mighty warrior." And that message set Gideon on a course where he was lifted out of the hole and became the mighty warrior who led the people of God to defeat the Midianites and get good bread back in everybody's hands.

Threshing wheat in a winepress is settling. It doesn't get you to the real thing. We, the people of God, who live in the midst of so much promise, can actually settle for way less than the real thing. Over and over and over. It can become normal. That is why we can have such trouble understanding our breaking points. That is the ache—the ache for the real life Jesus holds for us.

In small ways we take our eyes off Jesus and settle for the idols of the land we live in. It is subtle. It's like Coca-Cola Life. *This is pretty good*, you might say. But it's good only if you haven't had the real thing in a while.

Enough about Coca-Cola. When you taste the real thing in life, you will be willing to throw everything else away. It will be a breaking moment to do that, but if you allow it, it will be a breaking open.

Many of us have, for some time, been threshing wheat in a wine-press. We are making bread, sure, but there is something so much better for us. We have been drinking wine—some of us more than others—but there is a new wine.

We often wonder what Jesus meant when he promised abundant life, what some Bibles translate as "real" life (John 10:10 MSG). It leads us to ask the questions, What are we missing out on? What life is there yet for us to experience?

Are we reading stories with our kids anymore?

Do we go outside and see the sunset much?

Do we laugh deeply with our loves anymore?

We are doing a lot of stuff, we are alive—but are we settling? God loves us so much that he will find us in our holes and offer us the real thing.

Who wants to stop hiding in a cave making subpar bread? (Are you raising your hand with me here?)

Also, do we want real life? Would we even say yes if God said, "I have more for you"? Or would we say, "Well, Coca-Cola Life is pretty good." (I knew I couldn't stop the Coke metaphor.) Do we want to step into a spacious place to make some good bread? Do we want some new wine that wasn't made in something with the chaff of wheat in it? Or do we want to just be busy? A bit numb? Rushed? To just get through life? Because that's an option.

No matter what your zip code is, it's not the promised land. We get to our promised land by listening to God. He speaks to us in our hunkered-down spots. He calls us mighty warriors. He calls us out.

When we stop listening to God, we settle for less.

The people of God in Gideon's day were living in the actual, bona fide, without-a-doubt promised land, and they stopped listening to God. God reminded them, "I delivered you from Egypt. I freed you from a life of slavery. I rescued you from oppressors. I pushed them out of your way and gave you their land."

Here's his message in Judges 6: "I said to you, 'I am GOD, your God. Don't for a minute be afraid of the gods of the Amorites in whose land you are living.' But you didn't listen to me" (vv. 8–10 MSG).

They stopped listening to God, and that's all it took for them to think, *That god over there looks good.* And that god offered some good things for them culturally in that time. But not the real thing. They stopped listening to God, and then, all of sudden, they didn't farm their own land, they didn't live in their homes anymore, and just to get bread, they crawled down in holes that weren't made to thresh wheat. That's how it works for us. When we stop listening to God, we think, *That god over there looks good.* And the moment we do that, we are settling.

When we settle for less than life with God, we live in fear.

When we stop living totally dependent on God and start depending on other gods, we get really afraid. When we have fear in our lives, we should ask, *What am I dependent on?* Whether that god is your job or your kid, any other god leads to a life of fear. We live in fear because nothing else can deliver what the real thing can. We start hiding instead of thriving, and that is settling.

Most of the time, we don't know we are settling.

That's the hard part. The nature of settling is that you usually don't even realize it. You are just drinking Coca-Cola Life and thinking it is pretty good. I obviously cannot let this example go. It was a big moment in my life. (And if Coca-Cola Life is your beverage of choice, I am so sorry. Really. It has been discontinued and this must be a difficult time for you.)

Most of the time we don't know we are settling! It's one of the reasons I wrote this book. I want to point out places where we are settling for less. Because I did it. I settled. And I want to be done with it. God wants you to be done with it too. God is not good with us having idols that steal life from us. He designed us for real life to the full. Every time we give our hearts to another god, our hearts get divided. And a divided heart is settling for less than the one real thing, a singular devotion to Jesus.

But there is good news.

Once you see that you are settling, it is hard to forget that you are.

This is a really good thing!

It will feel uncomfortable at first. We will feel much discomfort when we realize it makes no sense to be in the hole we are living in while God is calling us out. Imitation of life can be comfortable. It won't be easy to just step out. At first, we will probably remind ourselves, and maybe even God, why we can't stop living this way. But we can't let the initial discomfort dissuade us from rising up.

As we walk this journey together and begin to rise up out of holes we've hunkered in for a long time, we are going to see clearly some truths that we won't be able to easily unsee. I hope it is hard for us to forget. I hope when we get lost in our phones instead of dancing with our kids, we remember. I hope when we are so tired because we've worked and worked and worked instead of resting in spacious places, our spirits are troubled. I hope that once we see these areas where we have settled, it will break us, break us open, to where we can't get it out of our minds that God is promising us more.

Don't settle for a substitute.

Don't settle for what you can protect. God has more territory for you. It's more than you can keep your arms around or put an alarm system on.

Don't settle for what you can determine. Some of us have settled for the life of what we can make happen. There's more and it's out of our control.

Don't settle for what you can explain or predict. You are smart, but there are thoughts higher than our thoughts and ways higher than our ways (Isaiah 55:8–9).

Don't settle for what you can see. If I am in a hole, then I can't really see all there is. So we can't live our lives based on what we can see right before us.

Breaking open is about letting God push back the barriers that we have made so we can have more. More bread. More wine. More life.

But to do that we have to say, "No longer will I settle for a substitute for Jesus." You can say it right now if you want.

No longer will I settle for a substitute for Jesus.

Sometimes we need a substitute for sugar. I understand that. Some of us use Sweet'N Low or Equal or Splenda or stevia, or some of us scrape sugar off a rock in our backyard or whatever the new thing is, but we understand that is a substitute. Right? We are settling. And we get used to it. And that's fine.

But with God we don't have to settle. We don't have to settle for less than full life with Jesus. We don't have to live life with a little less God or just some of Jesus. No.

We don't have to settle.

RISE UP TO REAL LIFE

Here's how to stop settling:

1. Resolve to rise up.

2. Tear down idols.

3. March into battle every day.

Resolve to rise up.

This resolution is about one thing and one thing alone. It is not about self-talk, self-help, or pulling yourself up by your bootstraps. It's about hearing God's voice and believing that who God says you are is who you really are, even when all the evidence you see points in another direction. The first step in not settling for less than what God has for you is resolving to rise up out of the hole because God has called you out with his very voice. God calls you a mighty warrior, and it will sound preposterous, foolish even, to anyone else listening. But we choose to believe it because we believe God's voice holds more power than anyone else watching our lives in the arena.

Believe him. Believe that your God, who created you, knows the real you.

Gideon did not consider himself great. Gideon did not consider himself tough. Gideon was hiding. He was hunkered down in a cave trying to make bread in a place made to make wine. He had one eye on his work and one eye on the Midianites. God said to him, "The LORD is with you, mighty warrior."

Hear it. "The LORD is with you, mighty warrior."

Resolve to rise up out of the hole. You have been breaking into bits down there. Up here you can break open to life.

When we hear it, we resolve to rise up. We are done settling. If God says we are mighty, we're going with God. The way God got his people back to the real thing was by telling them they were mighty warriors before they were really mighty warriors. Maybe it will work for us too.

Say it: "The LORD is with you, mighty warrior."

Look at your kids in the morning before they exit the car in the car line and say it to them: "The LORD is with you, mighty warrior." Look at your grandmother before you leave her at the assisted living home and remind her, "The LORD is with you, mighty warrior."

Let's hear it for ourselves and say it to the people we love. It's going to feel so silly. Because at first you won't see a mighty warrior in the mirror or exiting the car. But after some days, when we say it, we *are* going to see a mighty warrior standing there. And we will realize we have been settling for something less. The mighty warrior emerges from the life broken open.

Ezra is a little boy in my church. I met him shortly after his mom, Erin, had adopted him after a season of him being a foster child in her home. Ezra is small for his age, and with Erin, he was living in a new home in a new community after a past that was like living in a hole. Erin taught Ezra this line: "The Lord is with you, mighty warrior." Erin would say it to Ezra every morning. Then Ezra changed it a bit. Instead of saying the Lord is with *you*, Ezra started saying the Lord is with *me*. "The Lord is with me, mighty warrior!" Some days I say it the Ezra way. You can too.

Tear down idols.

As soon as Gideon got out of the hole, he started tearing down idols. God asked him to tear down the altar his father had set up to a god called Baal. Gideon did it (Judges 6:25–27).

Can you imagine being asked to tear down idols that your dad had set up? We need to imagine it—like the real, modern-day versions of it. We need to recognize the idols that were handed down to us and begin to believe that we could be the ones who will tear them down. I tend to think that I will be able to do something as drastic as tearing down generational idols only *after* I have proven myself— you know, after I have done some other mighty things. But that is not God's way. This is another paradox of faith. God will call us mighty *before* we have done anything mighty. We need to trust that the idols won't help us and remove the fake gods we have been relying on.

Let's begin to imagine fathers sitting down with sons and saying, "I've made an idol out of my job like my father before me, but no longer." Mothers telling daughters, "I made an idol out of seeking perfection. I am not passing that down to you."

This is powerful stuff, but it is delicate work. Let me offer a few questions that will be helpful in identifying idols and tearing them down.

FIRST, ARE YOU STALLING? Can you think of something you know you need to do but you just never do it? The answer to this question could point to an idol that needs to come down. If, like a nagging ache, you have a conversation that you know needs to happen, an act of forgiveness that needs to be offered, or a habit you know needs to die, that could be an idol that needs to be torn down. Good news: God is really patient. So if you have been stalling on something and you know it, there is still time.

My friend Kelly had lived her whole life feeling that her mom had abandoned her. We talked about it often. Kelly had found a lot of strength through breaking open. She had found space to heal, and even though full reconciliation would never happen with her mom, she had found a wholeness in life that she never thought she'd know. And then Kelly heard the news that her mom was deathly ill. It was like the Band-Aid was ripped off and she had this nagging feeling that she needed to offer forgiveness to her mom. Forgiveness was not "deserved" in this case, but God's love doesn't really work that way.

Kelly had no obligation to go. No one would have questioned her if she didn't. But she went. She drove five hours to Cleveland, and in the space of an interstate drive alone, she found peace. She entered the hospice facility, looked her mom in the face, and forgave her. She told her she loved her. Kelly held her mom's hand and sat by her side while she died. Kelly called me and I could feel the power coming through the phone. Now, Kelly would tell you she stalled for a while. She realized her difficulty in forgiving had moved from something that was understandable based on the circumstances to a sort of crutch in her own life. She had begun to lean on it. She had let unforgiveness become an idol. Kelly would tell you that there comes a time when you will choose either to tear down that idol or not.

Are you stalling? The answer to that question might show you something that needs to be done, something that needs to come down.

SECOND, ARE YOU MINIMIZING? By that I mean are you saying, *Thank you for the invitation to come out of the hole, God, but what you are asking me to do sounds really dramatic. It will have huge ramifications.* Sometimes we take what God is asking us to do and we bring it down a notch or two. This is what Gideon did. He did tear down his father's altar to Baal. But he did it at night—when no one was watching and no one would know who did it.

Gideon knew that tearing down the idol would have big ramifications, so he made God's plan just a bit less than intended.

We all do this. We hear God's call to life, but we know that the steps to get there, the breaking it will require, will cause a ripple effect we aren't quite ready for. So we minimize what God has asked and keep the settling thing going for a while.

Galatians 3:3 asks, "After beginning by means of the Spirit, are you now trying to finish by means of the flesh?"

Look at it for a second. How many times do I begin something by means of the Spirit? God is doing something big and asking something big of me and I say, *Thank you, God. I'll take that from here and finish it out.* When we do that we start with the Spirit and finish with the flesh. We finish it out under our own power—with what we can do. That is minimizing.

Jesus said, "I want you to have abundant life" (paraphrase of John 10:10).

And I reply, *Thanks, God. I'll take it from here.* And what I do is accept a mini-life. God is offering biggie size, and it sounds too big for me.

Are you minimizing? Have you taken God's big, beautiful dream for your life and minimized it, minimized it, minimized it until it is almost unrecognizable? Well, I've got more good news for you. God's plan prevails anyway. Yep, eventually God is going to get God's way. We may lose some time—and who hasn't lost some time? But God's plan ultimately is not held up because of us. The truth gets out. But we might miss out. "Many are the plans in a person's heart, but it is the LORD's purpose that prevails" (Proverbs 19:21). I can stall, but God's will will be done.

Are you minimizing? Good news: God's plan prevails.

After Gideon took down his dad's altar with a headlamp on in the middle of the night, and in the morning everybody saw that the altar had been obliterated, their conclusion was that Gideon must die (Judges 6:30). The lesson here is that other people don't like it when you tear down idols because they are their idols too. That leads us to question number three regarding identifying and tearing down idols.

THIRD, ARE YOU IN DANGER? One of the biggest deterrents to tearing down idols is the trouble we likely will face. All this warrior/battle talk may be hard to grasp for most of us who are not daily in a physical conflict involving real armor and real swords. Let me be clear, though: if you start tearing down idols, you will put a lot at risk.

When we resolve to rise up and choose the Jesus life, not the one handed down by culture or families, there will be the feeling we are in danger. It will feel like breaking.

Are you in danger? Good news: you are not alone.

The Lord is with you, mighty warrior—but it's not just you. When we take on the breaking-open life, we find deeper connection with other people, not less. While we fear losing people by going deeper with God—and in some ways that does happen—there is richer communion with others that can never be experienced when we are hunkered down in isolated winepresses.

Tearing down idols requires clarity, courage, and community. First you have to see the idols; identify where you are settling. It also requires courage—that's the resolution to rise up rather than stay down with what you inherited from your father's altars to false gods. And it requires community. We find community in the church to keep walking and ultimately march into battle every day.

March into battle every day.

When my youngest daughter started school, it just wasn't her thing. Like a lot of new kindergartners, she had some anxiety about entering that big school building, but Phoebe's was less like anxiety and more like disdain. She didn't *like* it.

I had the pleasure of being her chauffeur every morning. I got to take someone where they didn't want to go. We had a routine. Her elementary school had two buildings, one for the upper grades, where her sisters went, and then another for kindergarten and first grade. Our routine began after we dropped off her sisters at the A building and rounded the corner to see the B building. It is here that Phoebe took a deep breath and said every morning upon the sight of her school, "Welcome to the torture chamber." After this proclamation I would reach back with my hand and we'd say a prayer together, the same prayer every morning:

> Oh Lord, this day we thank you for our lives and we commit our lives to you. We thank you for our sweet Lord Jesus who gives us passion and purpose. Lead us this day to be faithful to you and to each other. Forgive us of our sins and renew us to life in you. We believe by faith that you alone will sustain us today. Help us to be a light to other people and hold us safe until we are together again. In Jesus' name, amen.

After the prayer we'd play a game where I held on to her hand as she tried to wiggle free. Phoebe always won just as we eased up to where a teacher opened the car door for her to get out. She'd say, "I love you, Dad."

I'd say, "I love you, too, Phoebe."

She'd say, "Don't forget to wave."

I'd say, "I never forget to wave."

Then she'd step out and, before walking into the school, she'd turn and face me like a soldier leaving for war. With an expressionless stare, she would lift her hand with a nonmoving wave/salute as she prepared for what to her felt like battle.

We love telling that story, but all joking aside, school was hard for her. She eventually transitioned into saying "Welcome to the Pit of Despair" after watching The Princess Bride.[3] But all her humor was covering the fact that walking in that place every day took about all she had. It felt dark to her.

One day my wife, Rachel, received a phone call in the middle of the school day and it was Phoebe. You don't expect your kinder-gartner to call you. Phoebe was having a tough day and her teacher let her call. Tears were streaming down her cheeks as she choked out the words that she wanted to come home. She wanted to come home bad. Rachel told her she couldn't come home. But what Rachel did say has become a mantra in our family and even in our church. Rachel said, "Three more hours. You can do this. You are brave. You are strong. You are known. You are loved, little girl."

You see, Phoebe's brilliant teacher didn't let Phoebe call Mom so she could go home or get instructions on how to behave. She needed to be reminded of who she was.

The Lord is with you, mighty warrior. Brave. Strong. Known. Loved.

Hearing that is what gets you out of the hole. We resolve to rise up because of who God says we are. Then, every day, we set about the work of tearing down idols that distract us and want to put us back down in the hole. And every day, we march into battle. We take steps into a world that is hard and holds risk. But we can't hunker down any longer because we have been called to this battle. In this battle is the life we long for, ache for, and have been made to live. We weren't made for hunkering down in self-protection any more than wheat should be threshed in a winepress.

But we will need a routine for readiness each day. And we will need some people we can call to remind us of who we are.

So, let's review.

- You don't have to settle.

- Here are some signs we are settling:

  - We have stopped listening to the words of God.

  - We are living fearful lives.

  - We are seeking out substitutes.

- How do we get out?

  - Resolve to rise up.

  - Tear down idols.

  - March into battle every day.

- Some questions for awareness about idols:

  - Am I stalling?

  - Am I minimizing?

  - Am I in danger?

A question to consider when walking into battle: Do I have a routine to prepare me for the battle awaiting me? Do I have a person on speed dial I can call to remind me who I am?

If all that seems like too much to ponder at this moment, let's ask ourselves this: Are we ready to stop breaking down in our hunkered-down places and ready to rise up and break open, out in the open in a way that could save us?

Gideon made a ton of mistakes. We see that his faith really wasn't all that strong. Well, it was strong some days and not so strong on others. Sound familiar? But he got out of the hole. God got him out of the hole. God pulled him out of the hole with truth about who he was, who God saw him to be.

Over time there may be places that you used to see as scary that become places you walk into confidently. That's what happens when we break open. It allows light to pour onto darkness, and the darkness runs away.

Three years after kindergarten I have seen a change in Phoebe. She started asking me to pray before we even reached the car line. She was speeding up the truth infusion. We don't play the hand game anymore; she's in the third grade after all. There was one day, I can't pinpoint the exact time, when she stopped saying, "Welcome to the Pit of Despair." She just let it go. She hasn't said it in months.

The school is the same place. The same stuff happens there. She just sees it differently. She's on the student council and she is working to make the school a great place for all children. She ran on the platform of listening well to students about their needs and advocating for them (that and better cafeteria desserts). And sometime this year she started walking confidently into the school without turning to give me the solemn-face wave. As she walks away, I hear the sound of footsteps marching into battle.

Brave.

Strong.

Known.

Loved.

Rise up.

The Lord is with you, mighty warrior.

four

DESPERATE, NOT DRAMATIC

We are all desperate, and that is in fact the only state
appropriate to a human being who wants to know God.
Having fallen from the absolute ideal . . . we have nowhere
to land but . . . in the safety net of absolute grace.

PHILIP YANCEY

Constant drama will wear us out.

But with more space to breathe, standing now on the ground instead of hunkering down in a hole, the broken-open life chooses desperation instead of drama.

I'll explain.

Once we get some space and rise up, we will not find ourselves immediately in a place of freedom. First, we will feel exposed. Because, well, we are exposed. No longer do we have the fast pace that masks how we are really doing. No longer do we have our bunkers, which, though it is hard to breathe down there, gives us the illusion of protection. Quickly we will find ourselves longing for the old pace and the old cave because we don't know how to live in this new, wide-open space. It all will initially feel unsafe and uncomfortable.

The best way to describe it is *dramatic*. It will feel dramatic. And so our first inclination will be dramatic action. But before we act, let's take stock of where the need to move is coming from. We will need to move. We will need to act. What is required of us, though, is not a *dramatic* reaction but a *desperate* one.

There is nothing inherently wrong with drama. There are some moments that require a dramatic or exaggerated action. Don't mishear me and get bogged down in thinking that all drama is bad. There are times when extreme action must be taken to bring good attention to something or someone that is being neglected.

I am making a distinction between drama and desperation here so we can talk about the difference between the intense action we take that keeps our focus on us (what we will call drama) and the intense action that leads us to be dependent on Jesus (desperation).

This is the next step in breaking open, and it is critical. It's the place where it is easiest to stall out, to retreat to the comfort of your pace or cave. This is the place where so many stop their journey and never really encounter the hope, healing, and wholeness that is available in this life.

The tendency to stir up drama at this point is a natural and common one. We lash out. We make some noise. We excessively complain until someone notices. We do things that are about being seen and heard, which is not bad, but it also leaves us without seeing and hearing God. Our internal noise creates so much external noise that no one, including us, can hear where God is moving us next. What is required is just one tiny step different from drama, but the distinction could save us. What we need is to get really desperate.

Drama (the kind we are talking about) puts a focus on self.

Desperation is dependent on and focused on someone else.

Drama is all show and no go. (Think the social media post we make that gets a lot of comments but doesn't help anyone move forward.)

Desperation has an aim.

Drama will wear you out.

Desperation will save you.

SOMETHING ABOUT THAT NAME

Recently our church hosted a funeral for a neighboring church. Our two churches began sharing space with each other some years back as a way of seeking to expose some racial division in our community and work toward healing and deeper relationship. Our church is predominantly white; our sister church is predominantly black.

We were hosting a funeral for one of their congregation members who had died unexpectedly, a young dad leaving his wife and daughter behind. The man who had died had also been a childhood friend of mine. We grew up just a couple of streets apart from each other, and, when we were little, he and I were assigned to the same seat on the bus in elementary school. His name was Letai. What I remember about Letai is that he, a sixth grader, was kind to me, a first grader. He was the biggest kid on the bus, and I was the smallest—and that's why the two of us shared the seat while others sat three to a seat. We enjoyed our unlikely pairing. I remember over time feeling safe and comfortable in Letai's presence. And now our journeys crossed paths again in his untimely death.

Letai's community was grieving his death greatly. Hundreds and hundreds of people came to the funeral service; it was the largest funeral I've ever attended. There was a palpable grief in the air. An audible grief. In fact, the grief became so overwhelming, so loud, that I wasn't sure how we would get folks calmed down enough to have the service. I was not the pastor for the service; I was standing in the sound booth in the back of the room, seeking to be a good host as we shared our space. So I watched closely what Bishop Bobby Sanders, their pastor, was going to do.

Bishop Sanders is a mentor and hero to me. I have learned so much from him over the years about grace, strength, and courage, and I was looking to see what he would do now. First, he read some Scripture to give meaning and comfort to the moment, but the grief was so heavy that nothing seemed to penetrate it. It set like a cloud over the room and began to push us down as we asked hard questions in our breaking hearts.

Then Bishop Sanders began to softly and repeatedly say one word. Well, one name. *Jesus.*

Jesus. Jesus. Jesus. Jesus.

He said it over and over.

Somehow that name began to quiet and focus the room of seven hundred suffering lamenters. The wailing began to subside and heads began to lift.

Jesus. Jesus. Jesus. Jesus.

I'm not sure how others experienced this moment, but here's what happened to me.

I felt like the name of Jesus pushed me against the back wall. Just hearing his name spoken caused my heart to become sensitive to what I was really feeling. Tears dripped down my cheeks. *Jesus. Jesus. Jesus. Jesus.*

I became keenly aware that I often make Jesus something to think about, read about, and talk about an awful lot. But there was something about this palpable moment in the loss of a young life, a tragedy I couldn't explain, a multitude of emotions, that made me feel only my desperation for Jesus. I'd had a bit of space in my life, and I was feeling a bit exposed at that moment when the name of Jesus seemed to take hold of me. Years before, Jesus had captivated my heart, but for his name to take my breath away that day was quite a surprise. I realized I was desperate for him. For *him*. The aching and the numbness and the longing I'd often felt had a very clear aim, and it was Jesus. Like the grieving family, my only action toward healing in that moment was to desperately depend on him.[1]

Desperation leads you to be dependent. It has a purpose. It drives you closer to him.

Desperation has an aim. It won't be a dramatic post on social media. It won't be making sure people know the pain we are feeling. It won't be blaming or projecting or the drama created when we make it all about us. It will be realizing we are desperate and desperately aiming our lives toward Jesus.

Drama will wear us out, but *this keenly aimed, totally dependent desperation will be the rescue.*

This kind of desperation is a breaking in itself. It breaks us away from self-focus and self-promotion. It breaks us out of old habits of causing drama to distract us from what is really happening in our hearts. It breaks us open to really see our need for Jesus.

Here, though, is what it doesn't mean. Two things that I will call "not prerequisites" for breaking open with Jesus.

1. You don't have to have Jesus figured out.

Desperately aiming your life toward Jesus *does not mean you have everything figured out about Jesus.* People who fell at the feet of Jesus had different levels of religious background, theological understanding, and acceptance by the wider religious community. Their understandings of who Jesus was and what he could do for them varied widely. What they held in common was desperation! A woman who doctors couldn't fix, a father whose son was near death, a fisherman who knew he was not worthy to be in the Lord's presence (Mark 5:25–34; John 4:46–54; Luke 5:8). They all fell at Jesus' feet because they were desperate for what only he could provide.

The most common hesitancy I see in folks before they fully come to Jesus is they think they aren't qualified for some reason. They don't know the Bible all that well. They don't know how to pray. Their past intimidates even them. They don't really understand everything about Jesus. Well, good news! You will never have Jesus fully figured out. That's not really how love and relationship work, anyway. You need to know Jesus. But you won't have everything figured out about him. He still surprises me. I can think I'm as far down the road in loving Jesus as you can go, and then I can hear his name spoken in the midst of unspeakable tragedy and I realize he has something for me there. Even in my breaking. Don't wait until you have Jesus all figured out to fall at his feet.

The second "not prerequisite" is like the first.

2. You don't have to know the full implications.

You do not have to have everything figured out about what following Jesus means for your life. This is a big one! We are willing to break open to Jesus, but we wonder, *How is this going to affect my life? My marriage? My hobbies? My career? What's next?* When Paul had his Damascus road experience in Acts 9, he was on the ground before Jesus and wondering what he would do next since his encounter with Jesus had left him desperate. Well, Jesus said, "Get up and go into the city, and you will be told what you must do" (v. 6).

Did you catch that? Paul had to get up, and he did not know what was coming next. He had built his whole life around being an expert about God and what God wanted people to do, and now he was being led by his arm (because his physical eyes weren't working) and being told, "You will find out later what's coming next."

This may sound scary to you. I find it so encouraging. It means I can have a life-changing experience with Jesus and have no idea what I'm supposed to do for a while. I love that! Most folks I talk to who are eager about following Jesus into this new life don't know what that new life will look like. That's okay. Just get desperate. Lose the drama that puts all the focus and pressure on you. That kind of drama is exhausting, and it masks what is really going on.

DESPERATE HERE AND NOW

Here's the best way I know to break it down. It involves some words that end with the suffix -cy. Before you go to sleep on me or have flashbacks of middle school grammar, let me show you what I'm talking about. The suffix -cy means that you are in the state of something. It doesn't mean you are doing something; it means you are living there. It is all happening in real time. The pepper doesn't just have some spice to it; it is spicy. He isn't just incompetent; his incompetency is a state of being.

A few of these -cy words can help us understand why the difference between this desperation and drama is so important.

Desperation is about urgency.

This is not just an urgent matter; our desperation for Jesus leaves us in a state of urgency. We live there. We are constantly in urgent need of Jesus.

Drama isn't about urgency; it says everything is an emergency. But no one can live in a constant state of emergency. And when we are always manufacturing drama in our lives to cover what's really going on inside, we beckon everyone to join us in eternal emergency. This can't be sustained.

But life is crazy and filled with brokenness and grief, and that can lead us to live in urgency. An urgent need for Jesus, for real love, for real connection.

Desperation is about urgency. Drama is constant emergency.

Desperation is dependency.

Desperation says, "I am totally dependent on Jesus. I can't do it on my own. I can't do anything on my own. I am totally dependent; I live in a state of dependency."

For some of us the word *dependency* gives us caution, but it shouldn't. What we have heard warnings about is *codependency*, which is when people have too much emotional or psychological reliance on each other. The kind of drama that puts the focus on us leads to codependency; it sets us up to have unhealthy relationships. In other words, whenever we put all our dependency on anyone other than Jesus, we are going to create a lot of drama.

Dependency is acknowledging and relying on Jesus to be our deliverer day by day. Drama leads to codependency between people who weren't made for that level of reliance.

Desperation in Jesus leads us to find sufficiency and significancy.

Jesus said to Paul, "My grace is sufficient for you, for my power is made perfect in weakness" (2 Corinthians 12:9).

We'll never find a sense of sufficiency apart from Jesus' grace, and we'll find true significancy only when we let his power work in our weaknesses. If we use drama to cover our weaknesses, we will never fully know Christ's power. We'll feel insufficient because we'll be relying on our own strength and insignificant because our suffering will have no meaning.

We all feel insufficient and insignificant. But that's because we are often seeking sufficiency and significancy in the wrong place. *Sufficiency, having enough, is found in Jesus' grace, and significancy is found in Jesus' power.*

But true sufficiency and significancy is found only when we can see, understand, and acknowledge our weaknesses.

Let's look at a bit more context on Jesus' words to Paul found in 2 Corinthians 12.

Paul wrote, "Three times I pleaded with the Lord to take it away from me. But he said to me, 'My grace is sufficient for you, for my power is made perfect in weakness.' Therefore I will boast all the more gladly about my weaknesses, so that Christ's power may rest on me. That is why, for Christ's sake, I delight in weaknesses, in insults, in hardships, in persecutions, in difficulties. For when I am weak, then I am strong" (vv. 8–10).

Paul had some kind of issue. He called it his thorn in the flesh (v. 7). It was some problem, some compulsion, some wound that caused him pain and that he couldn't get rid of. Three times he asked God to take it away. He pleaded. *Take it away from me. Take it away from me. Take it away from me.*

For centuries scholars, Bible teachers, and students of Paul and the New Testament have tried to figure out what in the world Paul was talking about. What did he mean by the thorn in his flesh? What was it?

Some say it was a lingering temptation, others a chronic eye problem, migraines, epilepsy, a speech disability maybe. Some think the thorn in his flesh was another person. We don't know what Paul's thorn was. It was just always there, bothering him, hindering him.

Most of us know what ours is—the thing that is sticking in our sides and causing us constant, lingering pain.

What is your thorn in the flesh? What's its name? If you are having trouble thinking of yours, ask, *What is it that I have pleaded with God to take away and yet it remains?*

When I was thirty years old, I was diagnosed with a permanent blockage of the main vein in my right arm. It's called thoracic outlet syndrome. It's caused a lot of change in my life. I have pleaded with God to take it away. It remains.

Even more troubling to me is a general anxiety that I have had since I was a little boy. I have tried everything to shake it. It remains.

Take it away, God. Take it away, God. Take it away, God. These things remain.

We all know what it is like to have a lingering issue that makes us feel really weak and to ask God, *Is there another way?*

There is another way.

It is not the dramatic way of constant emergency, codependency, and insignificance.

It is the desperate way. We acknowledge, "Yes, I have suffering in my life, but I will not let it drive me away from God. No, instead, it will drive me closer to Jesus and the things of God."

Paul said, "Three times I pleaded with the Lord to take it away from me. But he said to me, 'My grace is sufficient for you'" (vv. 8–9). Paul's pleading, his desperation, led him to hear the voice of Jesus saying, "I am enough for you."

I love that Paul didn't tell us what his thorn was. If I had known Paul's thorn, I could think, *Well, I don't have bad eyesight* (or whatever it really was), and move on. The mystery of Paul's thorn allows me to look at the place in my life where I am weaker than weak and hear Jesus say, "Yes, Jacob, my grace is enough for you. Enough for your panic attack. Enough for your numb right arm. Enough for it all."

And Jesus can say to you, "My grace is enough for your loneliness. Enough for your temptation. Enough for your desire to take the next drink. Enough for this difficult moment. My grace is enough for you!"

Jesus is saying, "I have enough. Enough for your weakest, most desperate place. It is not outside of what I can cover. My strength is made perfect in your weakness."

Don't miss this secret. Don't miss this gift. Don't miss this foundational part of breaking open to Jesus. God's strength is made perfect in your weakness. Not your gifts. Not your bragging points. Not your beauty, favor, money, or strong place. In your weakness. God's strength is made perfect in your weakness. Can you imagine?

Everything else is a weaker strength than the perfected strength of Jesus in your weakness.

Anything other than you saying, *I can't do it without you, Jesus*, is weaker. If you choose any other path, you will be weaker. Your strongest place is realizing that you can't do it without him.

Our significance is not found in getting rid of our weaknesses but welcoming Jesus into our weaknesses. That's why we must do this breaking. In the breaking the weakness is exposed, and that's where the power comes in.

Here, Paul got a bit dramatic—but a good kind of dramatic. He reasoned that if Jesus was in his weakness, if Jesus was in his suffering, then he was going to talk about his weaknesses and suffering so Christ's power could come upon him.

Paul said, "Therefore I will boast all the more gladly about my weaknesses, so that Christ's power may rest on me" (2 Corinthians 12:9).

We are looking for power. The power is found when we say, "I can't do it anymore," and we start boasting in that. And that sounds, well, desperate!

So how do we get there?

We plead with God in our pain.

We don't ignore the pain. We turn toward God in the pain—not away. Paul asked God not once, not twice, but three times. He pleaded with God in his pain. We may need to do some pleading right now! To get real with God is to get real about the pain, and the path to power is actually pleading with God in it.

We start believing Jesus is enough.

This is tough. We have to say it: "Jesus is enough."

We hear it, but to believe it is to say, "This relationship is wearing me down, but Jesus is enough."

"I don't know if I can make it through this semester, but Jesus is enough."

"I'm angry with someone I'm going to see at the family gathering, and on my own strength we are going to have a blowup. But Jesus is enough."

Jesus is truly enough. You start saying it and you start believing it, and that's where the power of God comes into your weakness. It's to believe so deeply in Jesus that just hearing or saying his name brings you back to power.

We let God's power come into our weaknesses.

Sometimes we hold God out of our weaknesses. That just leads to drama. Opening ourselves up to his power in our weaknesses is a turning point in the broken-open life.

And then comes the crazy part.

We start boasting in weakness.

Paul started boasting and delighting in weaknesses. Delighting in insults. Delighting in hardships. Delighting in persecutions and in difficulties. It sounds crazy, but this is one of the truest true things I have ever experienced. When we are weakest, we are strongest.

We all have our struggles. We all have a thorn in our sides.

Christian teaching does not say that we will not suffer with our struggles and thorns. It does not say that we can pray everything away. What it does say is "When I am weak, then I am strong." And the only way to discover this strength is to get really desperate before Christ.

In the next chapter we'll take another step toward healing and power. But I promise you, if we keep walking around with Jesus as if he is something we should attend to every once in a while—instead of the person who is the desperate aim of our entire lives—then the healing will be only in part and the power will not be fully magnified. This kind of power and healing comes to weak people who brag about how weak they are outside of Jesus and how they find true power in him.

THE PRACTICE OF FASTING

I've found that a really practical way to step out of drama and into desperation is to fast. Fasting is a way to intentionally step into desperation for God while skipping all the drama. Fasting, or giving up something for the purpose of growing closer to God, is a quiet, weakness-exposing, often hidden, nondramatic way to stay broken before God and find lots of power. Those who fast see their drama quotient reduce and their desperate need for God increase.

Most of us haven't considered fasting, at least not for spiritual reasons. (Fasting for health reasons and weight control and loss is quite popular now.) So this could be a moment when you tune out a bit, because you don't think you are spiritual enough for this type of practice. If you feel like tuning out, lean in for just a few minutes more. It could be really worth it.

Richard J. Foster wrote, "Fasting can bring breakthroughs in the spiritual realm that will never happen in any other way."[2] Foster said this from his own experience, but he also was clearly referring to something Jesus said.

In a moment when Jesus' disciples were asking how Jesus accessed a power that was way beyond what they had been able to do, he pointed them to the way to that power. A boy had been healed by Jesus of impure spirits. The disciples couldn't drive the spirits out, but Jesus could and did.

They said, "We tried that and couldn't do it."

Jesus said, "That can only happen through prayer and fasting" (Matthew 17:17–20, paraphrase).

It's interesting how seldom people of faith talk about fasting when it seems almost all our heroes of the God story fasted in a way to show their desperation for God. Moses fasted. David fasted. Elijah fasted. Esther fasted for her people and her nation. Daniel fasted. The prophetess Anna, awaiting the Messiah, came to the temple each day and worshiped and fasted. Paul fasted. Jesus fasted.[3]

Jesus fasted.

When? At a moment that could have been his breaking point.

Why? As a way of being ready for what God had for him next.

That's why I am asking you to lean in here. If you are experiencing brokenness and really (or desperately) want to know what God has for you next, then you should look to Jesus here.

The story is found in Matthew chapter 4. "Jesus was led by the Spirit into the wilderness to be tempted by the devil. After fasting forty days and forty nights, he was hungry. The tempter came to him and said, 'If you are the Son of God, tell these stones to become bread.'

"Jesus answered, 'It is written: "Man shall not live on bread alone, but on every word that comes from the mouth of God"'" (vv. 1–4).

Jesus fasted.

Jesus was hungry.

And when the devil said, "We can make some bread right here," Jesus said, "Man shall not live on bread alone." Jesus was actually quoting an old verse from Deuteronomy (8:3). The verse was from a time when the Israelites were hungry, but strangely it says God actually caused the hunger so the people would know they didn't live on just bread.

Spiritual hunger can take place in physical aches. And our physical aches can point us to a reminder that we really live on what God gives us, not just on bread.

Jesus was more prepared to encounter the temptation of the devil because of his fast, not in spite of it. Jesus was not weaker or more vulnerable to the Evil One's scheme; he was readier. Another great paradox! This is astounding. Jesus was able to withstand this temptation because of his decision to fast. Fasting leads to some spiritual breakthroughs, and it happens when we are weaker in the flesh but stronger in the spirit.

Intermittent fasting that we do for weight loss or control actually strengthens you metabolically. Our organs are working better because of the restraint and removal. Same thing spiritually. That's why I'm spending so much time here. Not because I expect everyone will take a forty-day fast from food. (I've yet to do that!) I hope you'll see how restraint and removal can make us readier for what is coming. This can't be ignored!

The devil tailored his temptation to Jesus' method of going deeper with God. And he will do the same with us. As we seek to go deeper with God, as we pray and seek and even fast, the devil will come right to us—right to this place of us seeking God.

Jesus decided, "I'm not eating bread to go deeper with God."

So the devil said, "You want some bread?"

You say, "I want to break open. I want hope and healing and whole-ness in my life."

So the devil will say, "You will just break down" or "You are foolish to think you will find strength in this place." He will tempt you to find strength somewhere else—somewhere else in a drama-filled life.

The devil has no new tricks! This is the same thing that happened in the garden. In the beginning, in the book of Genesis, God essentially said, "I have what you need to eat—just don't eat *that*" (paraphrase of 2:17). God was calling the first people to restraint so they could experience the fullness of life. And the people in a place of restraint, which was based on obedience to God's Word, were tricked by the devil to eat the one thing God said not to eat. And that created a terrible mess. A mess of sin, a return to chaos.

And the devil wants the same thing to play out with us. He wants us to retreat back to our caves and back to our pace to try to outrun the pain.

Fasting and Desperation

A fast pulls us back to desperation for God.

A fast says, "What I need most is God."

I think there are some things that don't happen until we get desperate for God. I also think people can spend their whole lives without a desperation for God and miss so much power.

I get these ads on social media for a company that helps people fast for weight loss. (It freaks me out. Why am I getting these?) The ads show a split screen. On the left is a guy about my age with a protruding belly. The guy on the right's belly is much trimmer. The left is the before; the right is what is experienced after fasting.

I wonder if my spiritual belly is more like the bigger belly. Rarely am I starving spiritually. All day long, I consume many things—news, social media posts, texts, even spiritual books and devotions. But they don't really fill me up; they bloat me.

The breaking-open path shows us that taking some things away will be what actually fills us up.

We don't live on bread alone but on every word that comes from the mouth of God.

Dallas Willard said, "Fasting confirms our utter dependence upon God by finding in him a source of sustenance beyond food. . . . Fasting unto our Lord is therefore feasting—feasting on him and on doing his will."[4]

Again, the purpose of all this fasting talk is not to convince you to be like Jesus and give up food for forty days. It's meant to make you consider what you could do intentionally to turn your heart desperately toward God so you will be prepared for what is next.

If we are serious about this path, let us consider a few kinds of fasts.

A Non-Food Fast

This means taking something away for a period of time. I'm going to let you think on what that could be for you. Perhaps it's social media or screen time. Maybe a distraction that creates drama or more focus on self. To really break open instead of breaking down, try intentional removing and restarting that is done unto our Lord.

A Fast You Didn't Choose

Maybe something already taken away can become a fast for you. This is something I have been thinking about lately. Another way of saying it is, maybe a frustration can become a fast.

I had a recent consultation with my doctor where he recommended I give up caffeine for a season. I wanted a new doctor. But I have had the same doctor for twenty-five years. I trust him. So I gave up caffeine. Until then I'd been having a cup of coffee or two a day, with pretty much no breaks, for about twenty years.

Three weeks into no caffeine, I was a terribly unhappy person. No one wanted to be around me. I realized, as I was in the midst of studying about fasting, that at no time in that three-week period had I thought about my doctor's no-caffeine edict as having anything to do with the Lord. It was just a frustration. And it was a big one.

It was then that I decided, really out of desperation, to try to think about my no-caffeine life as a fast unto the Lord. And very quickly, I found power. Now the restraint was connected to my spirit. Now the weakness in the flesh started to feel like power in the spirit.

What can you think of right now that has been a frustration? Something that has been taken away, maybe something that is leading to your breaking, could turn into a fast unto the Lord.

Fasting and Your Ache

Let your ache lead to a fast.

Hopefully this book has helped you think about the aches that you are sitting right on top of. Maybe this book has helped you go a little deeper into your ache—not just dipping your toe and feeling the ache every once in a while but really trying to feel it and see what it means.

That ache is really a longing for Jesus.

And that's where fasting comes in. When we pull away simple distractions, maybe even needed sustenance (like food) for a time, we can get to the bottom of the ache. It is there that we find that we are aching for Jesus. And he meets us right there.

Remember:

- You don't have to have everything figured out about Jesus to take the next step.

- You don't have to have everything figured out about what it will mean for your life.

- You just have to be desperate for him.

We begin to think in terms of

- urgency, not constant emergency;

- dependency, not unhealthy codependency.

We find sufficiency and significancy, and we find it in weakness and desperation.

So we plead with God in our pain.

We believe Jesus is enough and let him come into our weaknesses.

We actually start boasting in our weak places.

And it's there, in desperation, that we begin to experience the freedom of the new place God has for us. It's there that things long shrouded in darkness are seen in the light. It's there that things long blurry come into focus. It's there that we begin to see clearly. And that's what we will talk about next.

five

CLARITY, NOT
CERTAINTY

We are not necessarily doubting that God will do the best for us; we are wondering how painful the best will turn out to be.

C. S. LEWIS

Breaking open means being certain
about less.

I'll let that sink in.

Breaking open means being certain about less but gaining clarity
about more.

Brokenness in our lives leads us to less certainty.

We question God.

We question ourselves.

There aren't easy answers.

We feel that we have been so deconstructed that there aren't even
materials left over for the reconstruction.

That's why the way we break is so important. Breaking leads to
less certainty, but breaking open can lead to more clarity. When
we break open we hold fewer things for certain and, by gripping

less tightly, we actually begin to see our lives and our purpose with clearer vision. The journey of faith is not one where we know exactly what the next step will be, but because we hold desperately to God, we are actually more confident about moving forward.

So if you are questioning in the breaking, doubting in the breaking, or maybe even holding a hopeful wonder about the future, you just might be able to see things more clearly than you ever have before.

———

Charlotte had always reminded me of Jesus.

Now, she was sitting in my office crying. Sometimes, as a pastor, I sit with folks who pray with unexpected, surprising tears. It's like a dam breaks and they get to do some grieving that they have desperately needed to do, but they hadn't given themselves permission until the pastor meeting. Fresh tears that have been held back for way too long flow down cheeks and onto the carpet.

That's not what was happening with Charlotte. These weren't new held-back tears. She had been crying for six straight weeks. Her tears were life now. Her tears were not like a dam that had burst but like a steady river from an unending source. Her eyes were overworked, tired, and swollen.

Charlotte had always reminded me of Jesus, and now here she sat in forty days of tears.

Her first words surprised me. She said, "I don't believe Jesus is grieving with me." She asked me what I thought. A person who reminded me of Jesus was grieving and was asking me if I thought Jesus was grieving with her. I knew I had to choose my words carefully.

When I say Charlotte reminded me of Jesus, I just mean that I always felt God's presence when I was around her and her family. Her husband, Eric, and her son, Ezra, and especially her daughter, Ellie, seemed to carry with them the fragrance of Christ. Ellie was in second grade, and she had grown up in our church and always loved to be held by her mother in worship. During the songs, she sang and worshiped with all her expressions and all her heart. You could just feel it. People turned their heads and watched the little girl and Jesus communing together. When I watched Ellie in the arms of Charlotte, who seemed to be in the arms of Jesus, I felt closer to God. They reminded me of him.

Charlotte had grown accustomed to crying for more than a month because her sister, Molly, had died. We had prayed for Molly for years. For her brain tumor. For the cancer. We had prayed for her healing and for a miracle. Molly and Charlotte had been living together ten years ago when the cancer first came. It was Charlotte who had taken Molly to her appointments. Charlotte who cared for her, many times staying up through the night. And now after a decade of good news and more bad news in excruciating intervals, Molly had died, and Charlotte sat in my office with a lot of questions.

Charlotte was calm, but she was mad. She was sitting upright, but she was aching. She was confused about God and confused by God.

She told me she felt like her body had a wide, gaping hole in it. A hole that sucked everything in and everything out of her, making everything feel empty.

She told me about a sculpture called *Melancholy* by Albert György. It is a sad metal figure sitting on a bench, and the figure's whole body is actually a hole. You see right through him. She showed me a picture of *Melancholy* on her phone. We sat in silence and looked at it for a while.

As I said, I knew I had to choose my words carefully. I ended up choosing not to say much. No declarative statement seemed to fit the moment. Charlotte had always seen her future with Molly, and now that future was gone.

This Charlotte seemed less certain about everything. She wasn't "light in her eyes" Charlotte. She wasn't "worshiping joyfully with her daughter" Charlotte. She was "barely hanging on" Charlotte. She was "breaking before my very eyes" Charlotte. Charlotte, whose faith had always inspired me, was now in that place where the very foundations of her faith were shaking. She was coming to me, I realized, not for answers but for help. Answers can help, but there can be help without answers. That's what she was looking for.

And then I realized that, in some ways, Charlotte was breaking in that moment. She was not breaking down; she was breaking open. Charlotte's pace had finally slowed after many weeks of preparing for Molly's death and all the things you have to do after a loved one dies. If you have been through this, you know it brings an exhausting, unrelenting pace. But once that pace slows there is just space. A terrible, numbing space, but a space nonetheless. She now had room to question and wrestle and pray, and she was doing that.

I saw that Charlotte was peeking her head up out of the cave. At this point just barely peeking her head up, but she was trying to see out. She had come to talk with me, and we were beginning to breathe the clean air present when you can get your head out of the chaff-filled winepress.

What was so clear to me was that, in spite of all she had been through, she was reaching out in desperation to a friend, her pastor, and, yes, to God. Space. Rising up. Desperation.

Charlotte and I talked about how much of Molly's death was beyond our understanding. Certainly (there I go using certainty) Molly's death did not fit any plan or hope or aspiration that we had. We acknowledged the uncertainty of it all.

We weren't certain why we had prayed and prayed for Molly and then she died. We weren't certain why she had to suffer so long. We weren't certain exactly how long the intensity of this grief would last for those close to her.

But our uncertainty was not leading us to despair or a loss of hope, no matter how much it may have felt that way. As we followed the uncertainty it was clearly leading us to God. Actually—and maybe surprisingly, if this journey of breaking open is new to you—we felt more clearly that God was with us, God's love was for us, and that Jesus and his resurrection were the one thing that would get us through.

This clarity is not without pain or mystery, but it is very real and very powerful.

TRUSTING A GOD WE DON'T ALWAYS UNDERSTAND

"As the heavens are higher than the earth,
so are my ways higher than your ways
and my thoughts than your thoughts.
As the rain and the snow
come down from heaven,
and do not return to it
without watering the earth
and making it bud and flourish,
so that it yields seed for the sower and bread
    for the eater,
so is my word that goes out from my mouth:
It will not return to me empty,
but will accomplish what I desire
and achieve the purpose for which I sent it."

(ISAIAH 55:9-11)

God's ways are higher than our ways. God's thoughts are higher than our thoughts. God's Word will accomplish God's desires and purposes. That's comforting. Most of the time. But when you face the starkness of some of the pain and brokenness of this world, this can also lead to a lot more questions.

For some of us it can lead to a sense of disillusionment. If God's ways are higher and he is accomplishing a purpose and that involves the death of my sister . . . well, that's where some of us tap out. *Check please! I got to go.*

There is another option. Rather than seeking to explain God (or tapping out), we seek to know God. And this happens when we let go of our search for certainty and instead seek clarity.

Certainty is about having the answer to the next question.

Clarity is about finding confidence to take the next step.

Certainty is about knowing more.

Clarity is about seeing better.

Certainty is holding tightly.

Clarity involves loosening your grip.

Breaking open leads to clarity and probably less certainty.

Less certainty doesn't mean we loosen our beliefs in God or about God. There are tenets of the faith that, by faith, we can be certain of. This is another paradox that is proven true as we move forward in life. But when we talk about our "beliefs" or core tenets of our "faith," we still use words that inherently point to a bigger-than-our-ways and higher-than-our-thoughts God. *Belief* and *faith* inherently mean that something cannot be proven with certainty.

It is proven with the clarity gained by faith. And this is way more powerful than any earth-gained certainty.

There aren't a ton of practical steps to this. There is really one big step, and it is less like intellectual assent and more like stepping off a cliff.

It involves us moving from one place to another. If you don't like the cliff metaphor (I don't, and it was my metaphor), let's try this: moving from seeking certainty to gaining clarity involves changing seats.

There may be a seat you are sitting in that is not yours to sit in. You're thinking, *I'm sitting in my recliner.* Metaphor, my friend—stay with me. There may be somewhere that you are sitting where, until you get up, you will be sitting in the wrong seat.

When my first daughter, Mary, was born, I stood over her and looked at her. They placed her in her mother's arms and my heart changed. It has never been the same since I laid eyes on Mary Elizabeth Armstrong. That moment changed my life. Changed the way I loved. Changed the way I thought. We spent a few moments with Mary, and then the nurse came and said, "We will be taking Mary to the nursery now."

And with that different heart, with that different sense of responsibility, I was like, "What? You can't take her already!" We had waited nine months for this baby and now nine minutes later they are taking her away. (That may be an exaggeration.)

The nurse explained this was how it worked, and, seeing my struggle, she said, "Why don't you walk with me?" She rolled Mary down a hall in a cart as I followed after them. We turned a corner and walked through a long, covered walkway that went over a road below. I walked just a few steps behind, watching this nurse, who for all I knew could be some kind of covert spy baby stealer. I didn't know.

Let me take your baby.

Uh, maybe not.

We came to the door of the nursery, and she punched in a code on a keypad (spy-like) and I realized again she thought she was taking Mary away from me. But I walked close behind her, and that kind nurse let me come into the nursery with her and my baby. She cleaned Mary up. She weighed her. Ran some tests. It was so cool just to be with brand-new Mary. And then she put Mary in a big bed with special lights shining down on her little body. And the nurse was like, "You aren't leaving, huh?"

"Nope."

She put a folding chair next to Mary's bed and I sat down. I was tired. Don't you love stories where men talk about being tired after their wives have been through twenty-seven hours of labor? I don't think I've even said Rachel's name in this story.

I sat there, and after a few minutes I looked up and realized I was behind the glass. You know where family members come to see their babies? I was sitting behind that glass. Different family groups were looking in, pointing and smiling at their new family members, and there I was. Grown man with stubble on his chin and exhaustion in his eyes. I was too tired to even be embarrassed.

Right about that moment, I felt a buzz in my shirt pocket. It was my phone signaling a voice mail. I took a listen and it was a guy from my church named Tommy, a guy a bit older than me with girls of his own. He said, "Jacob, congratulations. She's beautiful. I'm outside of the glass looking in at you."

I looked up. There was Tommy. But I kept listening. This is the part I remember word for word.

"Her every breath in and her every breath out are out of your control. You can't make her breathe." And then he said, "So stand up, walk away, and come out here with the normal people."

And I did. Because I was sitting in the wrong seat. Not out of bad intentions, you see. Out of love. Out of responsibility. Out of fear. But I was sitting in the wrong seat. It was not my seat to sit in.

I wanted to be certain of her next breath. Certain of her future. Certain of my ability to protect her. That was the wrong seat for me. The better seat for me was not in determining her steps but in being clear to whom I would entrust her.

There may be a seat you are sitting in that is not yours to sit in. It's quite likely, actually. Through all that life gives us, we often end up sitting down in a seat of control or shame or certainty. Some of us have grown quite comfortable in the seat of cynicism or anger. Those seats and many others all have something to do with not allowing God to be God. Those seats are about thinking our ways and thoughts are on par with his.

JESUS TURNS THOSE SEATS OVER

There is a famous story about Jesus turning over tables in the temple (Matthew 21:12–13). Somehow we always miss the part about the chairs.

You may have heard it. Jesus entered the temple courts and drove out all the people who were buying and selling there. The temple had become a marketplace, and Jesus was none too happy about it.

Here's what was happening. God's people came to the temple to sacrifice animals. Over time it became easier to buy and sell the animals right there in the temple courts. For this commerce to take place, there also had to be an exchange of money. Since people were traveling in from all over, they had different types of currencies. The money changers became a part of the temple market as they converted the currency (of course with a bit of an upcharge, I might add!).

Jesus arrived at this temple court, and there was livestock everywhere, tables set up with ancient cash registers, and money changers converting Greek and Roman currency into Jewish coins. It was a mess.

It's here that Scripture says Jesus "overturned the tables of the money changers and the benches of those selling doves. 'It is written,' he said to them, '"My house will be called a house of prayer," but you are making it "a den of robbers"'" (Matthew 21:12–13).

Most people love this story. I think it is famous because we picture Jesus having a temper tantrum. And we like it. Jesus got angry and acted on it. It somehow justifies our temper tantrums and we feel good about making sure people know Jesus got angry. In our self-righteous anger, during particularly unbecoming outbursts, we can think, *You know who else got angry? Jesus. Boom. Mic drop, people!*

Jesus got angry for sure, but this story is about much more than Jesus' temper. It is really the story of Jesus' aching heart. His Father's house had become filled with distracted people who forgot that the purpose of the temple was not financial gain. The temple was a place to connect with the heart of God. This happens through prayer, Jesus said, not through doves and coins.

So Jesus is famous for turning over tables.

But he also overturned seats.

Jesus "overturned the tables of the money changers and *the benches* of those selling doves" (v. 12, emphasis added).

Jesus made it so that those working in the temple couldn't sit back down where they had been sitting. I believe Jesus was saying, "There is a seat you are sitting in that is not yours to sit in."

The people in the temple court had become certain about how to connect with God. They had commercialized it, monetized it, and scheduled it. By turning over their seats, Jesus was inviting them, with a sense of urgent desperation, to leave behind certainty so they could see something more important more clearly.

Setting down certainty for clarity is a theme in the story of God's people. In fact, Jesus was clearly pointing back deeper in the story when he turned over the tables and the seats.

Travel with me for a moment. We will get back to our seats in a minute. But let us travel from these words of Jesus back to the prophet Jeremiah.

———

Jeremiah was standing at the gate of the temple. It was about six hundred years before Jesus, but he was right where Jesus would later be, some think it was even at the same time of the year as Jesus' table-and-seat-turning, at the feast of Passover. Jeremiah was standing just outside the temple and, just like Jesus, saw a scene that didn't match his conception of what should be happening there. He saw people who had forgotten. He saw a mess. Jeremiah asked on God's behalf, "Has this house, which bears my Name, become a den of robbers to you?" (Jeremiah 7:11).

When Jesus turned the seats over in the temple, he was quoting Jeremiah. They were both saying, "There may be a seat you are sitting in that is not yours to sit in. You have lost the plot."

Just 'cause you've got a seat doesn't mean it's the right seat.

They turned seats over and called the distracted people of God to pray. That's what the temple is about, Jesus and Jeremiah were saying.

The temple was all about the people of God meeting with the presence of God. The temple was God's place in the middle of their city. It was God in their camp. God in their family. God in their hearts.

This whole religion thing is not so we can say, "Whew! We have a temple; we are safe." It's not a place to come and figure out everything about God. It is so we can say, "We have a God who will get us through the wilderness and never leave us." It's not about certainty.

But the nature of walking through hard things is that we forget this, and we start setting up chairs all over the place.

Jesus and Jeremiah were asking people to move seats, and they did so with emphasis (remember, I said sometimes dramatic action is needed). They were reminding the people of God that their seats are ones that look desperately to God, not ones that figure out a system to barter their way through their spiritual lives.

We aren't made to figure out God all the way, to have certainty about all God's ways and thoughts. We couldn't contain all of him even if we tried. And we can't have the right coins to get the right doves to make everything right. We can't know all about how God works, but we can know God. Clarity, not certainty.

Being certain can get you in a lot of trouble—because you can't be certain about everything. If you insist on pursuing certainty you will grow more and more rigid and, without knowing it, you just may box God out of the temple he truly wants to reside in—you.

Anytime we try to put God in a box, or a building, or a temple, we find out that God is bigger.

If you can handle one more biblical time travel, Jesus and Jeremiah were actually pointing back even further to where the temple idea came from in the first place. That started with David.

———

Jesus pointed back to Jeremiah six hundred years before him, and Jeremiah pointed back to David four hundred years before that. After some years of moving God's presence around in a tabernacle (a tent they set up every time they moved), the people of God had finally arrived in their own land. Then had their own new king, David, and David got an idea.

"Here I am, living in a house of cedar, while the ark of God remains in a tent" (2 Samuel 7:2).

David had plans for a building project. And God's response was really interesting.

God said, essentially, "I've never needed a house before now. I have been moving with you wherever you go. Did I ever ask you to build me a house? David, I took you from the pasture and put you on the throne, and I've been with you every step of the way. I have cut off your enemies, made your name great, and planted your people in a good land" (vv. 8–11, paraphrase).

Then God went on to say that he would build David a house (vv. 11–17).

We want to build God a house to keep him safe and confined. And God says, "I will build *you* a house." Really.

"The LORD declares to you that the LORD himself will establish a house for you" (v. 11).

When David received this word from God, the next thing he did was go and sit before God.

"Then King David went in and sat before the LORD," and he prayed (v. 18).

Why does this matter? God had the king of the nation step off his throne, come into his presence, and sit down before him. And pray.

David eased off his throne and went to another seat. The right seat. The seat of desperation before God.

Some of us need to get out of our current seat and get to a seat before the Lord.

There is a seat we are sitting in that is not ours to sit in.

We sit in the seat of king or queen of our lives, like we have it all figured out. We sit in the seat of control, the seat of fear, the seat of judgment, the seat of shame. We sit in the seat of smoldering anger. These are not our seats to sit in.

This is the time to stand up, walk out, and, instead of trying to control everything with perfect certainty, become one who gazes on what God has done in wonder and awe.

God wants us to remember it has never been about us getting a full grasp of him, somehow assenting with our minds to get up to where he is. No, it's about the living God coming down to be with us.

This might call for a moment of repentance. To say, "I'm sorry. I got it messed up."

Repent and believe.

Believing that Jesus was raised from the dead—that's how we get saved. Belief is never about perfect certainty. It's about faith. "If you declare with your mouth, 'Jesus is Lord,' and believe in your heart that God raised him from the dead, you will be saved" (Romans 10:9).

Believe today. Pray today.

Turn to God today. Turn from your sin today.

Get out of your seat today.

Ask God to show you if you are in the wrong seat right now.

Ask him to give you clarity about who he is and how much he loves you.

Remember, his ways are higher than your ways, his thoughts are higher than your thoughts, and that's a good thing (Isaiah 55:8–9).

Certainty is about having the answer to the next question.

Clarity is about having confidence to take the next step.

Certainty is about knowing more.

Clarity is about seeing better.

Certainty is holding tightly.

Clarity involves loosening your grip.

And now I'll add one more.

Certainty puts us in the seat of God.

Clarity puts us at the feet of Jesus.

———

A month or so after Charlotte came to see me, crying in my office, she came back to church on a Sunday morning. That's a really hard thing to do after a great loss like a divorce, or a job loss, or, in Charlotte's case, the death of a family member. Because you'd come to church before that happened and likely asked for a different outcome. Maybe even pleaded with God for that. So to step back into that place can feel foolish, or at least sad. But people of faith come back to the temple to worship—not because God is held captive there but because God desires to meet us there. He creates space for us there. He makes it a house of worship and connection.

Charlotte came back, and as I saw her worshiping, with Ellie standing on the chair next to her, singing praise to Jesus, too, I wasn't certain of much in that moment. But I could see clearly— well, almost clearly, through a tear or two—that God's ways are higher than our ways, and there will always be stuff here that I won't understand. I could see clearly that those unexplainable things don't have to be barriers between God and me.

All the emotions we feel in brokenness don't fall flat to the floor, but instead travel like arrows to the heart of God. He can handle the anger and the sadness and the confusion. He welcomes it. As we break open to God, our hearts open to the heart of God. He meets us there in the sorrow, in the pain. God helps us get out of the seat of determining our future and leads us to entrust our lives, our deaths, and then our lives again to him.

six

HOLINESS, NOT HAUGHTINESS

One way to define spiritual life is getting so
tired and fed up with yourself you go on to
something better, which is following Jesus.

EUGENE PETERSON

I was sitting at the kitchen table when my wife, Rachel, walked in.

You have to understand that Rachel first caught my eye in Mrs. Hibbett's kindergarten class at First Baptist Church. Before this sounds too weird, we were both in kindergarten. I've known my wife since we were three years old. We carpooled to preschool together. We went to the county fair together. We worked on high school projects together. We grew up together. For my whole life she has been a faithful friend, my biggest supporter, and my greatest love. She is undoubtedly 1,000,000 percent my all-time favorite person.

I was sitting at the kitchen table and she sat down after who knows how many days straight of us running hard. Not too much space and a whole lot of pace. But her sitting down was intentional, purposeful.

But.

I.

Didn't.

Notice.

I noticed her, but I didn't notice what she was doing. She was trying to slow us down so we could connect. Why didn't I notice? All I could think of was myself. My pace and lack of space had squeezed out my ability to notice. To notice my love.

I ended up saying stuff that hurt and hindered what we both really needed: connection. I didn't say any words that would be remembered months later. I just didn't say much of anything, because my heart was set on, well, *me*. My heart was hunkered down.

When Rachel sat down I was really tired, really hurting, questioning my ability to handle it all, which tends to lead me to question my worth. Then, without fail, I will end up hurting somebody else. And this time, it was not just somebody else—it was my person, my Rachel.

It's weird to me because this situation sounds like the perfect recipe for a big humility stew. Fatigue, insecurity, and brokenness should lead me to see my need for God. These sound like carefully selected ingredients for a situation in which I start to see my need for him, see my need for others, and cry out for help. It sounds like the table is set for humility, feeling low down but seeking the good way that leads to being lifted up.

But often that's not what the ingredients cook up. Instead, fatigue and insecurity lead me to lash out, say stupid stuff, and then shut down. When I should shrink, I puff up. Geez.

The things that should lead to humility actually tend to lead to a cocktail of self-righteous pride and self-pity that leads to hurting the very people we care about most. That happens when we have no space, live down in the hole, and create self-focused drama. It happens when we are certain that we are the ones who need the credit and attention rather than seeing clearly that Jesus is the one to whom we should divert our attention. (That was my best attempt at a recap of the previous chapters, if you just skipped right to this chapter. But seriously—who would do such a thing?)

Being really tired. Or really hurt. Questioning your ability to handle all that is before you.

Questioning your worth. Yes, that may sound like the path to humility.

It is not.

As strange as this may sound, these common indicators of our humanness don't lead to humility; they lead to heartbreak.

You end up moving from the kitchen table out to the front porch alone, wondering how you can be such a jerk to the person who loves you most. Which leads to more hurt and more questions. More hiding.

That kitchen table example was not hypothetical. You may have picked up on that. Did it happen the night before I wrote this? Perhaps. Mind your own business! (Breaking open isn't something that happens one time and then you move on to a perfect life. It's a continuous breaking and a continuous opening.)

We are now in an especially hard part of breaking open. We have already talked about several opportunities for us to intentionally break open in a way that leads to hope and healing and wholeness. But what I will describe here is more than intentionality. It is living differently.

HOLINESS IS MORE THAN HUMILITY

I could have called this chapter "Humility, Not Haughtiness." (More on haughtiness in a minute.) And humility is key, but what will be required from us next is not just an intentional mindset but a purposeful pursuit of holiness. To be what God is calling us to be. To be God's.

I really did think of calling this chapter something different. Because who wants to read about holiness? Who talks about holiness? My great fear is that this is the chapter people will skip. And I get it. When they see the word *holiness*, they will imagine people in long dresses who don't drink alcohol. I mean, I'm out on both accounts.

Holiness sounds scary. It sounds like something we can't do—just another list of things we won't be able to live up to. Rules we are destined to break. This is a misunderstanding of the holiness God is calling us to.

Holy is who God is.

Holy means set apart for God.

Holy is set apart with God. Different, but more than that—different with a purpose.

God offers to us an opportunity for new life, a second birth. In this new life we commit to living with a different purpose. The healing found in breaking open will be fleeting without a commitment to live differently.

Holiness is saying, "I commit to live differently, according to a new way. A better way. A more fulfilling way."

Every breaking-open moment in the Bible was sustained when people like Moses, Esther, and Paul chose to live differently moving forward. To live holy because God is holy.

So this chapter is not titled "Humility, Not Haughtiness," which would have been fine; instead, it is "Holiness, Not Haughtiness" because the pursuit of holiness will be the key that unlocks true, open, above-the-ground life.

Haughtiness condemns; holiness sets you free.

Haughtiness is not a word we use much. Or I don't. I think if I had an English accent I would, but alas, I don't. I would also use the word *alas* if I had an English accent. Even though I don't use the word *haughtiness* much, it's the best word for what we are talking about.

Haughty means you think you are superior *and* you act like it. If we are honest, we often think we are superior to others. We think in many ways we are better or smarter or "more right" than others. (Even spell-check has this problem; it says "more right" should be "righter." Well, I'll show you, Microsoft!) Thinking we are superior is one thing; acting on it is doubling down. And that is called haughtiness.

Holiness is a church word for sure, and it's about trusting, knowing, and living within the truth that we are set apart by God for his purposes. It doesn't mean following a certain list of right behaviors. It definitely leads to changed behavior, but it starts with an action by God that only he can do. God calls us and makes us holy.

So haughtiness is thinking you are superior and acting like it.

Holiness is knowing God has set you apart and acting like it.

Haughtiness will condemn you.

Holiness will set you free.

By *condemn*, I mean push you down, put you down, back in the wine-press, back in the hole, back in the cave where the walls fall in on you. That kind of *condemn*. Please don't overlook this.

We need to see and hear Jesus saying to us, "No matter what you have done, no matter how you feel right now, I have a new way for you. It's a holy way. It is holiness."

It is real freedom, real flourishing, living connected to what you were designed for. Jesus will give it. He's serious about this. Check this out.

The book of John tells us, "At dawn [Jesus] appeared again in the temple courts, where all the people gathered around him, and he sat down to teach them" (8:2).

This verse has a couple of clues that are important for us to understand this day. "At dawn" makes us wonder, *What happened the day before?* And "appeared again" makes us wonder, *When was the last time Jesus appeared in the temple courts?*

Here are the answers: Jesus appeared in the temple courts the day before, and he was being condemned. In John 7 he was teaching in the temple courts and was ridiculed, called demon possessed, and almost seized. A warrant for his arrest was issued and Jesus slipped away. At dawn, he appeared again in the temple courts. And now, the day after being condemned, he came back. The people there gathered around him, and he taught them.

This is where the story takes a sudden and surprising turn. If you've never heard it, hang on.

The teachers of the law, the ones who tried to condemn Jesus the day before, had a new target for their condemnation. They brought in a woman who had been caught having sex with someone who was not her husband. That's right—they brought her in to Jesus' classroom-in-progress, right there in the temple courts.

She had been caught in the act of adultery, which is when someone who is married has sex with someone who is not their spouse. It is one of the Ten Commandments: do not do it (Exodus 20:14). The teachers of the law caught her doing it, which assumes there was another person involved, a man, but they brought only her. They weren't trying to be holy; they were being haughty, trying to make a point.

And "they made her stand before the group" (John 8:3).

That part gives me chills. With whatever she was wearing when she was caught in adultery, they made her stand before the group. The verse makes me not only feel angry toward the teachers of the law but also think of how I could do something similar when calling someone out. (Lord, help us not make people stand before the group when they have been caught in sin.)

Clearly Jesus was not pleased with this.

This is an uncomfortable story. When I teach on it, people give me that look that says, *Really? They did that?* and *Really? We are going to talk about it?*

It is an uncomfortable story, but life is uncomfortable at times. *Haughty people like us do foolish things that we think will expose someone else's sin, when really we are exposing our own.*

The teachers of the law reminded Jesus what should be done to such an adulteress. They said that, in their law, Moses commanded such women to be stoned. To be killed by stones thrown at her. They asked Jesus, "Now what do you say?" (v. 5). And the scripture says, "They were using this question as a trap, in order to have a basis for accusing him" (v. 6).

Wait a second. They were using the question ("What do you say, Jesus?") as a trap. That means the woman's condemnation was not their main purpose. If the question was a trap, the woman was a prop. This story is usually thought of as a moment of condemnation for the woman. And surely she was being condemned. But she was actually just experiencing collateral condemnation. The tip of the condemnation arrow was pointed at Jesus. They brought the woman as a way of condemning him (again). They didn't care about this woman at all.

Again, they didn't bring the man she was with—maybe he escaped them, maybe he was a risk to fight back and ruin their trap, or maybe he was one of them.

What Jesus did next went down in history. It is the reason I am painstakingly going over the story with you now. But before we look at it, we need to really understand the moment. Jesus' reaction is incredible, but the context makes it even more astounding.

The moment was an interruption for Jesus. It is not uncommon for teachers to be interrupted or surprised. Ask any classroom teacher and he or she will tell you that interruptions happen all the time. As someone who teaches multiple times a week, I have grown accustomed to crying babies and ringing phones. I was starting a funeral sermon recently and someone's phone went off with the ringtone "Devil Went Down to Georgia" by Charlie Daniels. Not uncommon where I'm from. (My church is in Mt. Juliet, Tennessee, the hometown of the late, great Charlie Daniels.) I have had people fall out of their chairs, pass gas, and pass out during my teaching. There have even been a couple of heart attacks. A teacher has to know when the moment says *press on* (unintentional flatulence) and when you have to change course (paramedics come in).

Jesus was guest teaching in the temple courts. He was on point number two or in the middle of a great illustration when the actual teachers of the church came in holding a woman caught in adultery. They referred to their law and said she should be killed. They asked Jesus, "What do you say?"

Ready for this?

Jesus didn't say anything.

He bent down and started writing in the dust with his finger.

He bent down and doodled on the ground in the dirt with his finger. He didn't react. He didn't answer them.

Well, they kept at him, repeatedly asking, *What do you say, Jesus? What do you say, Jesus?* Finally Jesus gave them a verbal answer. He suggested that the one who had no sin could be the first to throw a stone (John 8:7).

Jesus said, "You go first." The day before, Jesus had been in the place of the woman. They had been trying to grab him and get him to the firing line. Now they were trying to trap him more subtly.

When Jesus saw the woman brought in by the haughty hands of the teachers, he did not return haughtiness. He did not feel superior and act like it. He identified with the one being condemned, knowing of course that he was the actual one being condemned.

If you know the story, you know the most dramatic part of the scene. All the teachers of the law, starting with the oldest, dropped their stones and walked away (v. 9). Everyone did. No exceptions. Jesus saying "You without sin cast the first stone" is the ultimate mic drop, which led to all the stones being dropped. Everybody walked away and left Jesus and the woman.

A scene that started with Jesus teaching a crowd of people and then was interrupted with this shameful scene—the shame of the woman and the shame of the men condemning her—was now just two people. Jesus and the woman caught in adultery. And he was back with his finger in the dust.

Finally he stood back up and asked the woman, "Has no one condemned you?"

She looked around. "No one, sir."

And then Jesus shook the foundations of the world by saying, "Then neither do I condemn you. . . . Go now and leave your life of sin" (vv. 10–11).

"No one," she said. And Jesus, with no rocks in his hands, said, "I don't condemn you either. Go now, leave your life of sin."

Let's go back a few chapters to John 3. Remember when we looked at Nicodemus, the teacher of the law who made space for Jesus? Remember the super famous verse, John 3:16? "For God so loved the world that he gave his one and only Son, that whoever believes in him shall not perish but have eternal life."

Well, how would you like to be the verse after the most famous verse ever? It doesn't get noticed much. But it's equally important. John 3:17 says, "For God did not send his Son into the world to condemn the world, but to save the world through him."

Jesus' purpose is not condemnation but salvation. So no wonder he was not eager to lead a stoning in the temple courts.

So who is condemned, if not the adulterous woman? If not the haughty teachers?

For that answer, we need John 3:18, the next, *next* verse: "Whoever believes in him is not condemned, but whoever does not believe stands condemned already because they have not believed in the name of God's one and only Son."

Condemnation is outside of Jesus.

Condemnation is not found in Jesus. It is found outside of Jesus.

Paul said, "Therefore, there is now no condemnation for those who are in Christ Jesus, because through Christ Jesus the law of the Spirit who gives life has set you free from the law of sin and death" (Romans 8:1–2).

There it is. Jesus came to condemn sin, not us! He came to conquer sin, not us! He didn't come to crush us with stones; he came to crush the head of the Serpent.

He told the woman, "I won't condemn you. But go, leave the sin." He calls us out of haughtiness and to holiness. This is the path to healing.

If Jesus has not come to condemn you but to save you, meaning Jesus has the power to keep you from dying, then Jesus also has the power to change you. To turn you from sin. To make you holy.

"Neither do I condemn you" is not a free pass to sin. It is a free pass *from* sin. What a great paradox.

You see what I'm saying? Some take this to mean, *Whew, thanks for the free pass, Jesus. I'll just continue on my way.* But no—Jesus gives a free pass from sin so you don't have to live in it anymore. You can be different.

A DIFFERENT LIFE ON PURPOSE

When Rachel and I married, she promised—goodness, do you know what she promised?

"Will you take Jacob to be your husband? Will you love him, comfort him, honor him, in sickness and in health, for better, for worse, for richer or poorer, till death do you part?"

She said, "I will."

She promised to be faithful to me until one of us dies. I didn't take that as a free pass to do whatever I want. That would be called unhealthy, dysfunctional, and in some situations, even abuse. No, she said we were together no matter what, and I chose to live differently. Any other choice would be haughty.

Haughtiness will condemn you; holiness will set you free.

What Jesus was telling the woman is what he tells us. "Yes, I can keep the rocks from pounding you. You are saved from that. But there's more." When Jesus saves us from the rocks, he also invites us to *more*.

Leviticus 20. That's the Moses law the teachers of the law were referring to. Leviticus 20 is where the Bible defines and condemns adultery. There is a ton of evidence that adultery causes all kinds of punishment for all involved. But somehow we never get to the end of Leviticus 20, which is where we can see the promise and purpose behind living a holy, set-apart life for God. Somehow we see the punishment part and miss the promise part.

God said, "You are to be holy to me because I, the LORD, am holy, and I have set you apart from the nations to be my own" (Leviticus 20:26).

God's purpose is not for us to experience the punishment of sin; God's purpose is for us to be holy and to be his own people.

The holiness, the setting apart, is so we get to be called God's very own!

Whether we identify with the haughty teachers, the passive onlookers, or the condemned woman, the call is the same. Jesus is beckoning us to see ourselves in desperate need of grace. Neither the teachers, the crowd, nor the woman can escape the stones until they hear the call to holiness.

Jesus prayed this type of holiness over us. He prayed for us to be sanctified (John 17:17). Since I'm using church words, I'll just go all in. What does it meant to be sanctified? That we would allow God to save us entirely—not just from the stones. That we'd allow him to bring about a full transformation of our whole lives. This is breaking open.

May our hearts break open toward God, where we give him everything and he changes everything.

John Wesley, the founder of the Methodist movement, said this about sanctification:

1. God has promised it in Scripture.

2. What God promises, God is able to do.

3. God is willing to do it now. And . . .

4. God actually does this![1]

We marvel at Jesus saying "Go *now* and leave your life of sin." But who can do that? Who has done that—left sin?

If we are asking those questions, I'll ask some more.

If Jesus says I can leave my life of sin, do I believe that is possible? Do I believe it's possible that Jesus could fully save me? That I wouldn't text that person who is not my wife to meet up? That I don't have to follow the pattern of my father? That I won't hurt people with my words anymore?

Is Jesus just saving us from stones hitting us, or is there more?

There's more.

Thank God there's more. When you break open before God, you get a power that changes everything.

> The grace of God has appeared that offers salvation to all people. It teaches us to say "No" to ungodliness and worldly passions, and to live self-controlled, upright and godly lives in this present age, while we wait for the blessed hope—the appearing of the glory of our great God and Savior, Jesus Christ, who gave himself for us to redeem us from all wickedness and to purify for himself a people that are his very own, eager to do what is good. (Titus 2:11–14)

That echoes what we saw in Leviticus 20. We get caught up in the stoning part. And we live in an age when people are casting stones. But God has called us to be holy as he is holy so we can be his very own (1 Peter 1:16).

For those who want to, I offer you this prayer to pray with me.

Father, by the power of the Holy Spirit, I break open, lay down my haughtiness, set down my stones, and ask that you make me holy entirely, for the sake of your Son, Jesus. Amen.

HEAR THE STONES DROPPING

We prayed to set down our stones. I want to offer you a different exercise. Find a few quiet moments now, if you can, close your eyes, and try to imagine what it would sound like for the stones around you to be dropped. If you feel like you are the one on the ground right now with a group of condemners around you, know that we've all been there. Sometimes a season of darkness or burnout or messing up time and time again can make you feel like a group of people are surrounding you with arms raised, stones in hand. Sometimes it seems like one day those stones are going to hit your body. Some of us carry the bruises and wounds of rocks flung at us in fury.

Try to hear Jesus right now inviting the stones to be dropped. Hear them hitting the ground. Imagine what it would feel like to hear the stones hitting dirt instead of flesh. You can't believe it. You are left without bruise or blemish. Your whole body is shaking, but not from pain—from unmerited relief.

Jesus is now calling us to something different.

We will be different from this moment on.

There are good things coming. Finally, there are good things coming.

A new power. A new ability to persevere. And, soon, miracles.

seven

VULNERABILITY,
NOT CAPABILITY

There is a beautiful transparency to honest
disciples who never wear a false face and do not
pretend to be anything but who they are.

BRENNAN MANNING

I was born to breathe, but shortly after I was
born, I couldn't.

My parents found me gasping for air in my crib. I was hospitalized
and diagnosed with asthma. I was born to breathe, but I needed
help to pull it off. When I would gasp for air, my parents would run
to my bedroom to help me. Afterward they would try to sleep, but
it's hard for a parent to sleep when listening for the sound of their
child's breath. It's difficult when you know you aren't capable of
making your child breathe.

My mom says that even after my condition improved I would still
gasp for air. I had learned that the gasping sound my asthma made
also resulted in Mama coming to my room in the middle of the night.
So, according to Mom, sometimes I would intentionally make the
sound, even after I was healed. I wasn't really gasping for air; I was
pretending to gasp for air because that sound led to Mom picking
me up and rocking me back to sleep. I'd grow out of that, right?

Fast-forward twenty years and I was gasping for air again. It was
the summer after my sophomore year in college. I had my first

full-time job and first bank account, I had rented my first house with a bunch of buddies, and I had just bought a ring for the love of my life. My pace was fast. I was leaning headlong into adulting, a term that had not yet been coined.

I woke up in the middle of the night and struggled to breathe. But there was no Mama to be found. I couldn't catch my breath. My heart was pounding. I lay there for a few moments, but I couldn't slow it down.

I got out of bed and did not wake any of the six other young men crammed into that house. I got in my car and drove myself to the hospital. The only logical thing I could think of was that at the age of twenty I was having a heart attack. Makes sense, right?

I drove to the hospital in my college town and walked into the emergency room lobby, and there I saw a pay phone. (Note to you young'uns: pay phones were phones that were attached to walls and you could put coins in it to make a call.) I called . . . who else? My mom. It rang once. It rang twice. And I hung up.

That's when I began to think, *I'm crazy. This is crazy. What's wrong with you, Jacob?*

I felt so afraid.

I walked back out, got into my car, and drove around in the wee hours of the night in a complete panic. I gripped the wheel. Alone. And tried to catch my breath. I. Could. Not. Slow. It. Down.

I put on Tom Petty and resigned myself to dying while driving my Saturn around town.

The next morning I returned to my house, still breathing, still alive. My roommates were alarmed and told me my parents had been trying to find me. Mom and Dad had seen on their caller ID the phone number from the hospital in their son's college town, and they were looking for me. Oops.

They came and got me and took me to the doctor. My childhood doctor did all the tests, and you know where this is headed (but I didn't). The doctor told me my heart was fine, and my lungs were fine, and I wasn't having an asthma attack. He called it something different—an anxiety attack.

I was twenty years old and I was afraid. I was gasping for air and I needed help.

At the heart of anxiety is a fear. This fear, whether acknowledged or not, is that we won't be able to pull everything off. My anxiety, when it is traced back, is usually rooted in a realization that I can't do it all, achieve it all, and please them all. My body was joining the chorus of *Jacob, you aren't capable to meet all the demands*. My very breath was acknowledging that I wasn't going to have enough to pull it all off. I was trying to breathe when what I needed to do was cry—cry to God.

Why don't we take a breath right now? In and out. You will do that about fifteen times in the next minute, about three hundred times as you read this chapter, around twenty-three thousand times today, and this year you will breathe eight million times or so. This means if you live eighty years, you will breathe some seven hundred million times.[1] Breath in your lungs and breath expelled from your lungs. Life.

When we are afraid, though, we breathe more. Well, sort of. We take more breaths—rapid and shallow ones. These breaths take place only in the upper part of the lungs, not engaging the lower part, where the real breath comes from. So we think we are taking more breaths, trying to get more air, but actually the more you breathe like that, the less you actually breathe.

That's why I say we need a good cry. Remember that kickstart cry of our infant lungs in the delivery room? That kind of breath reaches to the uttermost part of our lungs. It's like jumper cables on a fearful heart. It is a slower breath, a more desperate breath.

Let's try a slow, deep breath. How about another? And while you breathe, I'll tell you about Joshua. And I'll tell you, in this place of acknowledging and facing our incapable places, how God makes us breathe again. He actually makes all our breaths happen. We aren't capable of doing it on our own. That realization can lead to fear or a new kind of vulnerability, a new level of it. And in that vulnerable place, open to God, we learn that we are capable. Amazingly capable, but not the way we thought.

Oh yeah—Joshua. Deep breath, and then Joshua.

Our introduction to Joshua is as a young man, when he was handed the reins to lead the people of God. The context clues in the book of the Bible that bears Joshua's name all point to the fact that Joshua didn't feel he was ready. He did not think he had reached the place in his life for the sudden responsibility that was just handed to him. Oh, and I missed a big detail. Moses had died. His mentor, boss, and leader was dead. Moses was everyone's leader, but Joshua had spent his life walking next to Moses. Now he was gone. And everybody knew, including Joshua, that he was now in charge. Joshua was the one who was tasked to lead, well, everything and everybody. That's adulting on a whole new level.

Thankfully God had something to say to Joshua.

He said, "Moses my servant is dead. Now then, you and all these people, get ready to cross the Jordan River into the land I am about to give to them" (Joshua 1:2). God told Joshua that, finally, after waiting decades, the Israelites were going into the promised land, and Joshua would take them. Not Moses, Joshua.

At this point I'm guessing Joshua was looking for a paper bag to breathe into. There is no doubt that Joshua started to breathe faster and shorter. He breathed more but got less air. To hyperventilate is to breathe faster, thereby expelling more carbon dioxide and inhaling less oxygen. Joshua probably felt light-headed.

Here's what caused that:

- *Grief.* He'd lost Moses!

- *Responsibility.* Sudden and unexpected.

- *Lack of preparation.* If we read Joshua's story in the Bible, we can clearly see he was the one for the job. (After all, he's got his own book in the Bible!) But Joshua knew something that the others couldn't see. He wasn't ready.

- *Incapability.* Joshua had watched Moses and seen his strengths, and Joshua knew he didn't have what it took. Joshua was to carry out the greatest task imaginable. The one his grandparents had told him Moses would do. Now Joshua was in charge.

These feelings are the same for us. If we could track the source of our fears and anxiety, we would uncover places of grief, responsibility too soon, a feeling of lack of readiness, and, yes, that deep sense that we don't have what it takes.

All of these factors are embedded in Joshua's story, but the reason I say with such certainty that Joshua felt this way is not because of what Joshua said or did but because of what God said and did.

God told Joshua, "Be strong and courageous" (Joshua 1:6).

"Be strong and courageous" is another way of saying, "Don't be afraid."

As Joshua put his head between his knees to get his breath back, God told him to be strong and courageous. Then God gave some more instruction and realized Joshua still wasn't hearing him. God said again, "Be strong and very courageous" (v. 7).

God started giving more instruction about the importance of

following his commands and then, yep, God said it again. The third time, he said, "Have I not commanded you? Be strong and courageous. Do not be afraid; do not be discouraged, for the LORD your God will be with you wherever you go" (v. 9).

Three times God stopped during the conversation to say, "Are you all right? Oh, you're not all right. Don't be afraid."

Well, you know who God says "Don't be afraid" to, right? Afraid people. If you have to tell someone three times in one conversation to be courageous, it means they are not feeling courageous.

Joshua was struggling with cold, hard, real fear. Joshua was insecure and sure he couldn't do what God was asking of him.

The people God calls usually see themselves as incapable. The ones to whom God says "Do not be afraid" are a veritable who's who of Bible heroes. Abraham. Moses. Elijah. Mary. Joseph.[2]

God's people feel fear. Fear is a normal, God-given emotion. Fear doesn't mean you have done something wrong. It often means you are being called to something new, something great, something powerful.

THE THREEFOLD PROMISE

God gave a threefold promise to Joshua.

   1. "I will give you every place where you set your foot" (v. 3).

2. "No one will be able to stand against you" (v. 5).

3. And, the best one, "I'm not going anywhere" (v. 5, paraphrase).

Part 1: "I will give you every place where you set your foot."

God was calling Joshua to take a new land.

Joshua thought, *I can't do that.*

God said, "I know—I'm going to give you the land!"

The place God was calling Joshua to, God would give to Joshua. This is a foundational truth from the Word of God we need to hear: Every good and perfect gift is from God. Every good thing you get will not be earned by you but given by God.

Not only is every good gift from God, but it also belongs to God. That's a whole new understanding of capability! Not our capability, but God's!

In James 1:17 we read, "Every good and perfect gift is from above, coming down from the Father of the heavenly lights, who does not change like shifting shadows."

In Psalm 24:1 we read, "The earth is the Lord's, and everything in it."

Good things come from God and belong to God. Here's why this is so important. When we get this mixed up and start thinking, *I am making good things happen* and *I am gaining good things*, our worth becomes wrapped up in the effort to make it happen, and our destiny becomes disappointment and fear.

Trust me. This is a foundational truth of the Bible. It is a promise. The good things in life are from God *and* belong to God. When we start seeing ourselves as the ones responsible for making it happen and as the owners of all good things, then we should go ahead and open up the door and pull up a chair for our old friend fear.

When God told Joshua he would give Joshua land, he was saying, "This isn't about you making it happen. This is about you walking in obedience to what I tell you to do."

This, of course, is not easy. We struggle with it because it is so easy to see our prospering and success as a result of how great we are or how hard we work. I affirm that you are great! But prospering and success is a gift from God. He wants us to breathe and live, and we won't be able to take a deep breath while we feel the whole world revolves around our ability to make things happen. The whole world doesn't revolve around our capability. The whole world is the Lord's and everyone in it. Every good gift is from God and belongs to God. And that's just the first part of the promise!

Part 2: "No one will be able to stand against you."

One of the reasons Joshua was afraid was that he knew there were bad guys out there. There were enemies who were not going to like him going in and taking the land. And God said, "No one will be able to stand against you" (Joshua 1:5).

Here is the truth for afraid people of God. Our enemies don't stand a chance against us. When we begin to think our enemies are more powerful than God, we are in trouble. The reality is *no enemy, in the end, will be able to prevail against God's people.*

Yes, I included "in the end." This is important. There will be extremely difficult moments on the journey. We will face stiff opposition. At times we will feel like we are losing. We will feel fear because we'll see how strong our enemies are. But in the end, no enemy can stand against us.

In Stephen B. Oates's seminal biography on the life of Martin Luther King Jr., he recounted a time when Dr. King had reached his end. He was breaking. King was the face of the bus boycott in Montgomery, Alabama, and was facing great opposition. His life was on the line. His family was threatened. Late one night he received a phone call with a furious voice on the other end. The angry caller said, "If you aren't out of this town in three days, we gonna blow your brains out and blow up your house."[3] Then, there was a *click*.

King walked the floor. He thought about all he had studied and learned, but nothing had prepared him for this. He wasn't ready. He didn't feel capable. He put on a pot of coffee and decided to quit. He couldn't do this to his family, but he wanted to figure out a way to quit without embarrassing himself. (Ever done that?) Then he heard a voice that said, "You can't call on Daddy now. . . . You can't even call on Mama now."[4] King then put his head in his hands and bowed over the kitchen table.

"Oh, Lord," he prayed aloud, "I'm down here trying to do what is right. But, Lord, I must confess that I'm weak now. I'm afraid. The people are looking to me for leadership, and if I stand before them without strength and courage, they too will falter. I am at the end of my powers. I have nothing left. I can't face it alone."[5]

It was then King said he heard another inner voice, say, "Martin Luther, stand up for righteousness. Stand up for justice. Stand up for truth. And, lo, I will be with you, even unto the end of the world." And Dr. Martin Luther King said God "promised to never leave me, never to leave me alone. No, never alone. No, never alone."[6]

It was on that night, a night when King was ready to quit, that he said for the first time God became real and personal. King was breaking open. He didn't give up. He didn't quit. A few days later his house was bombed.

We all face enemies. My guess is you have more than one formidable opponent right now. It might be divorce or depression. It could be an illness or a change you didn't see coming. For some of us it is mounting and overwhelming responsibility that feels like an enemy to our very lives and breath.

Take a deep breath and hear this: in the end, no enemy will prevail against you, daughter or son of God. That's the second part of the promise!

The third part is what Dr. King heard God say to him.

Part 3: God is not going to leave us.

He's just not ever going to leave us. God doesn't do that.

God told Joshua the same thing he told Martin. "I will never leave you" (Joshua 1:5). This is the one true promise for those who truly know peace. I have sat with folks facing the most difficult of circumstances. I have seen many who know real and abiding peace. It was not found outside of grief or loss or fear, but in the midst of those things. It was found in knowing that God promised not to leave. And God won't break that promise.

THE VULNERABLE WAY

No one has ever been able to talk anxiety out of me. As someone who knows that struggle in my bones in the middle of the night, still today as an adult, I can attest that there is no bumper-sticker slogan that can move me from fear to peace. But the breath of God breathed into my lungs can.

Knowing that God is as close as our every breath can change the situation and allow us to breathe again.

Those are the promises from God when we realize we are not capable of making everything happen or perhaps even capable of going on.

The promises were:

1. God will give us every place we set our feet.

2. No enemy, in the end, will be able to prevail against us.

3. God will never leave us.

These promises from God lead us from a reliance on what we can do to a vulnerability with God and other people. This vulnerability makes us able, like Joshua and Dr. King, to face formidable opponents and have victory. The victory is found in a way of living open, or vulnerable, that is attained in a simple yet profound way of faithful living—a way of life that God gave Joshua.

Know our story.

Keep God's commands.

Remind one another.

Know our story.

If Joshua was going to understand God's commission to him, he had to know his own story. "Keep this Book of the Law always on your lips; meditate on it day and night," God told him (Joshua 1:8). When God told Joshua to stay close to his Word and reminded him he'd be with him like he had been with Moses, he was keeping Joshua linked to the story.

I've packed this book with that story. Like Joshua, we seek to keep God's Word on our lips. We meditate on it day and night. This doesn't necessarily mean we sit quietly for hours on end, but it does mean we keep God's Word ever before us, always in our conversations, and constantly on our minds. We talk about it over coffee with friends, at the dinner table with the kids, and we think on it on our evening walks.

This constant connection to a story bigger than us, and people who have already walked where we walk, keeps us open. Knowing we belong to a bigger family and a bigger narrative leaves us vulnerable to how God could do the same things he did in Joshua's and Martin's lives in our lives. When we hear God tell Mary "Do not be afraid" when she faced a crisis point in her life, we can hear God saying it to us when we face ours (Luke 1:30). When we remember that what Esther first saw as a breaking moment in her life became the moment she was made for, we can believe that perhaps we were born for "such a time as this" (Esther 4:14).

Keep God's commands.

God told Joshua to meditate on his Word day and night "*so that* you may be careful to do everything written in it" (Joshua 1:8, emphasis added). Simply put, there is power found in being obedient to God's Word. Doing our own thing and operating under our own power are not the pathways to life. When we break God's laws, we find ourselves in increasing places of anxiety and incapability.

Who can do everything written in the book, though? None of us! No, not one (Psalm 14:1–3). But, with humble hearts and the willingness to seek to follow all God's commands, we keep ourselves in that vulnerable place where God gets to stay God and we get to enjoy the good gifts he gives us. On the breaking-open pathway, we don't let our inability to get everything right be an excuse for not living in the abundance of what God desires for us. Put another way, no one who has breathed deep in the Spirit will resort to the short breaths of self-sufficiency ever again.

So we not only receive God's promises as truth; we also seek to be obedient to his commands.

Remind one another.

We are forgetful. And so we need one another. To remind us, to point us to God, to nudge us back toward the truth.

We know our story, we keep God's commands, and we remind one another over and over of the truth found in vulnerability. We step away from the traps of self-sufficiency once and for all and desperately seek God together.

Vulnerability, not capability, is the way to life.

No one has shown me this more clearly than a kid named Lukas. In the hours after Lukas was born, he suffered a massive stroke, paralyzing his entire right side. It was five days before he was stable enough for the doctors to run the necessary tests to determine what had happened, and once they knew, the prognosis was not good.

Mike and Jenn, his parents, remember standing in a hospital hallway as a doctor shared that Lukas would likely never walk or talk and that he would have significant impairments.

They prayed that God would heal him. This is Jenn's description of this healing prayer: "I admit that the healing I prayed for in those first horrible days is not what we have seen. I wanted that instant, lightning bolt kind of change. But what we have received over these past twelve years is more like a gentle rain, steady, restorative, and sometimes messy."[7]

A couple of years later Lukas had another setback. Seizures began to escalate and couldn't be controlled by medicines. Lukas had major brain surgery. They spent weeks in the hospital and were released just days before Easter.

In the following months Lukas started to talk. He began to scoot around on the floor. When he was almost four years old, he pulled himself up to stand on Christmas morning.

Lukas, who today is sixteen, is now known for his remarkable spirit. He has an astounding capacity to love and to empathize. He laughs—a lot. He exudes joy.

When he was four and barely walking, he got away from Jenn and Mike at a friend's wedding. It took a few minutes to find him, and when they did, he was leaning against a woman they didn't know. His one good arm was wrapped around her and his head was resting on her. She had tears streaming down her face. Jenn didn't know what to say, but finally the lady said through her tears, "I was just sitting here feeling completely alone in this crowded room when this child came out of nowhere and took my hand and hugged me." There are a bunch of Lukas stories like that.

I know Lukas because I am his pastor. A couple of years ago Lukas didn't want to go to church anymore. Anybody ever have a kid (or a partner) who didn't want to go to church? Yeah. Lukas didn't want to come. He made it difficult to get there. Finally, in desperation one morning before church, his parents asked him, "Why? Why don't you want to go to church, Lukas?"

He said, "I don't want to wear a handsome shirt."

"A handsome shirt?" his parents asked.

He was referring to a button-up shirt, you know, tucked in. They said, "Oh Lukas, this is about a shirt? You can wear whatever shirt you want to wear."

He said, "I want to wear my Star Wars shirt."

They said, "Wear your Star Wars shirt!" Lukas has great parents.

I saw Lukas that Sunday morning and I complimented his shirt, further cementing in his mind that his mom was crazy to make him wear a handsome shirt. Then, for whatever reason in the way God works, I remembered I had my Star Wars shirt on—underneath my handsome shirt—that morning. I unbuttoned my handsome shirt a couple of buttons and showed him my Star Wars shirt. It surprised him. It surprised his mom and dad. I had no idea what was going on. But we all laughed. We laughed at how God still surprises us with good things. We celebrated together that we were part of the same story and the same family. Lukas could come vulnerable to church, to God, and his Star Wars shirt was welcomed. It was a reminder to Lukas and, heck, to me, too, that we aren't alone, at all, ever. In the midst of all the brokenness that is life, it was like a long, deep breath.

I knew Lukas before that day, but after that we became good friends. We have shared *Star Wars* premieres together at the movie theater with our families, and dogs' birthdays too. One of my favorite memories with Lukas was serving Communion together at church with our Star Wars shirts on. Lukas, because of his vulnerabilities and his honesty about them, has capabilities that I rarely see in anyone else. I would include his parents in this as well. They have an amazing capability to serve other people, to make people feel heard, and to empathize. Lukas is capable of teaching and inspiring young people in a way that captures their full attention and leads them to live differently. Lukas is one of the most capable people I know. He knows where he is incapable, but he has remained vulnerable, not shut off—which has led to power for life. Breath for him and for others. And when we start breathing in that way, we really start seeing what God is up to.

We are tempted, though, to take a different way—the way that is not vulnerable and open, and seems to come so natural to us. When I was twenty and had my first panic attack, my instinct, even as someone who had been loved well by really loving people, was to close up and turn in. To hang up the pay phone and circle the town alone. No one had to teach me to isolate and close off; I just went there.

Eventually the drive led me back home and help was waiting there for me. The same will be true for you. If we know and remember our story, we will be drawn back to a familiar place, the place where we are reminded that God will never leave us.

Maybe that's what this book is for you. Just a reminder. The lies you have been listening to will not prevail in the end. God has something more for you, something really good. Something that, one day looking back, you may even call a miracle.

All right, deep breath.

God is giving you every step you will take.

Another breath.

No enemy, in the end, will be able to prevail against you.

Another breath.

God is not going to leave you. Ever.

Breaking and breathing, and then . . . miracles.

eight

MIRACLES, NOT MANIPULATION

The most incredible thing about
miracles is that they happen.

G. K. CHESTERTON

Brian and Hollie, who are some of our best buds, told us they were adopting a child.

When they gave us this surprising news, we had many similarities and shared experiences. They had two daughters the same age as our two daughters. We went to the same church and the same schools and played the same sports. We swam in their pool. We don't have a pool, but I'm sure we contributed something to their lives. In our group of friends with Brian and Hollie we have watched our kids grow up—really, we've watched ourselves grow up—and it's been a strength to do all the life together. It feels like we have gone through it all—lost jobs, illnesses, graduations, promotions, demotions, even death.

Brian and Hollie had been approved to adopt a son from Ethiopia at the same time Rachel was pregnant with our third child, Phoebe. We followed their travels closely. We prayed for them and bought them baby gifts. We would even join them at our local Ethiopian restaurant as we dreamed about life with their new son and tried to learn more about his culture. (Don't miss out on the ful medames. It's spicy beans and you can eat them for breakfast. You heard me.)

I remember when they learned their new son's Ethiopian name: Tamirat Yishak. We would all try to say it correctly. We are Southerners. It was funny. With my limited language skills, I could recognize Yishak as the Ethiopian version of the name Isaac. In the Bible Isaac was the unexpected son to Abraham and Sarah, who were too old to have children. His name literally means "he laughs," meaning Abraham and Sarah laughed when they found out they were having a son in their old age (Genesis 17:17; 18:12; 21:6). They laughed with joy, with surprise, with wonder. We laughed thinking about Brian and Hollie traveling to the other side of the world to bring home a son—laughs of joy and surprise and wonder. Wondering what it would mean for our lives.

The name, Tamirat, though, was a new one for us. One night at the Ethiopian restaurant Brian asked the waitress what the name Tamirat meant.

The waitress said, "America."

Brian and Hollie thought that was strange, a son named "America." As they discussed it with the waitress, trying to overcome accents and language barriers, the owner of the restaurant came out of the kitchen trying to clear up the confusion.

He said, "No, no, no, you misheard her. His name does not mean 'America.'" He paused. "His name means 'a miracle.'"

Brian and Hollie decided to keep the name his birth parents had given him. Tamirat Yishak. We all call him Ty for short. He is our miracle.

Ty and my daughter Phoebe, now eleven, have grown up together since they were babies. They are both spirited and they have had many a disagreement and more than one argument over a toy. They laugh together, they cry together, they swim together (in Ty's pool). They get on each other's nerves. Sometimes they play for hours without noticing the passage of time. When our families are together, five girls and one boy (sorry, Ty!), it is a mess. Things get broken. We mess up the kitchen. Mud is tracked in on the floor. It's loud. It's life.

And, while Ty is just a normal part of our lives now, at least for us old folks, we never lose sight of the miracle, which happened right in the midst of our already full, messy lives. When Brian and Hollie, who seemingly already had all they would ever need, felt an ache. It was an ache in their spirits caused by the Spirit, and they broke open and brought home a son.

A shift in the broken-open life—okay, *the* shift in the broken-open life—is to expect miracles to happen. Before we are born again, we manipulate situations. We manipulate other people. We manipulate our lives in the hope that they will end up looking the way we hoped. Let's face it: the more junk we encounter in life, the more likely we are to try to make sure everything goes the way we want.

But, when we find space, in whatever pace we may be in . . .

When we climb out of the hole, and we rise up after years of hunkering down . . .

When we get desperate for God, not just dramatic about circumstances . . .

When we realize we can't be certain about everything, but we find clarity at the feet of Jesus . . .

When we leave haughtiness and pursue holiness . . .

When we choose vulnerability over capability . . .

And when we break, but break open . . .

We get to see miracles.

When our eyes begin to look for what God is doing, when we stop trying to control everything, we see that God is doing things that we simply cannot do.

I believe in miracles. I get that that is a loaded statement. I know you have seen people try to manipulate miracles from Jesus. And not just slick traveling preachers staging people standing up from their wheelchairs. Normal people like us, if we aren't careful, when we are in the midst of brokenness, will try to use Jesus as a cosmic bellhop who we hope will move our baggage from one place to the next. Miracles don't work that way. But Jesus is still in the miracle business.

If we are honest about our brokenness and our inability to manipulate the miraculous, we will begin to see what he is up to in our lives. It is always good, and it is always redemptive, and it is always outside of our control.

I got a phone call recently from a Canadian professor. Well, a guy who is a professor in Canada. I don't think he is Canadian. I think he is from North Carolina. But he teaches in Vancouver. He was writing a book on places where the church in North America is experiencing new life. What might be called miraculous growth in a time when many churches are on life support. He had heard about our church, Providence Church, and wanted to ask some questions.

The questions were what I would expect from someone writing a book on church growth. But then, at the end, he said, "I do have one more question to ask." He seemed almost afraid to continue. Then he said, "I've been talking to people in churches all over the country, big churches, small ones, and there seems to be one common factor." He had my attention, but he was still dragging his feet. He said, "They all seem to have experienced a miracle early on in their story. Have you all seen any miracles?"

"Yes," I said. And even as I said it, I was seeking to find disclaimers, just like him, so I didn't sound too weird.

I told him about how in our first year, I received a phone call in the middle of the night. I was a twenty-seven-year-old pastor, less than a year into starting a new church. It was my first middle-of-the-night call as a pastor. I paced the floor while I heard a panicked mom tell me her son and his friend had been in a car accident near where I lived. They were on a helicopter headed to the hospital. She asked me to come.

I arrived in the downstairs lobby of Vanderbilt University Medical Center while the boys were in surgery. I had been in this lobby several times during the day. It is a large, spacious room, open in the middle, with different levels where, during the day, there are literally hundreds of people packed in waiting areas while family members are upstairs in operating rooms. That night, there was one huddled group in a darkened corner—the parents of two boys who attended our new church. We learned that both boys, Michael and Doug, were in serious condition. I was there when we learned that Doug's neck was broken and he was paralyzed. I was there later that week when they told us he would never walk again. It was that day in the trauma unit when Joe, Doug's uncle and legal guardian, asked me if I would ask God to heal Doug.

In that hospital room I looked at Doug, who was a few weeks from high school graduation, now lying motionless with a big contraption around his neck, beads of sweat on his brow, a grimace on his face. I really didn't have the faith in that moment to ask for him to be healed, but his uncle had asked me, and so I went to a sink and put water on my hand. I had heard about anointing with oil, but I thought water would have to work. I made the sign of the cross on Doug's forehead and somehow, vulnerably, knowing I wasn't capable, managed the words, "Doug, I anoint you in the name of Jesus, and pray that you would be healed." I asked for a miracle that I knew was so far beyond my control. He didn't move a muscle.

Some weeks later they moved Doug from Nashville to Atlanta to a center that specialized in spinal injuries and paralyzed people. I visited Doug there. I remember him flirting with the nurses and struggling to move his legs. And then some weeks after that I was standing up front at Stoner Creek Elementary where our new church was meeting. (Yes, Stoner Creek. I know. Stay focused.) I was standing up front beginning my sermon, when I looked up and there was Doug. He was walking down the middle aisle with the use of a walker. The small crowd of people in attendance rose to their feet and applauded. They cheered. Our miracle. God's miracle. Doug was walking again. Our community had been broken over his condition. We had questioned. We had cried. And now we rejoiced.

I told the professor, "Yes, there has been a miracle or two."

OUR STORY IS ONE OF MIRACLES

In the book of John in the Bible, when the author, John, wanted to tell the story of Jesus, he decided to situate the whole ministry of Jesus around seven miracles. John used the word *miracle* or *miraculous signs* twenty-four times, making miracles the pillars on which he built the story of Jesus.

The first miracle was at a party. Jesus turned water into wine (John 2:1–11).

The second involved a royal official begging Jesus to heal his almost-dead son (4:43–54). Jesus said, "Unless you people see signs and wonders . . . you will never believe" (4:48). And he healed the man's son.

The third miracle happened near a place where people believed miracles could happen. There was a pool, and if the water in the pool was miraculously stirred, the first one in the water (usually the fastest or strongest) got the miracle. Jesus walked past this scene, a pool of water surrounded by all manner of physically and spiritually broken people hoping they would make it to the water first. Jesus approached a man who had been paralyzed for thirty-eight years. The man, who had no chance of being the fastest or the strongest, told Jesus he couldn't make it to the pool when the water was stirred. With a word, Jesus healed the paralyzed man. Without a hospital or weeks in a center for spinal injury, that man stood up and walked (John 5).

I'm not going to do all seven miracles. You can find them in John's book in the Bible. But the story of Jesus is filled with miracles. Miracles for people who had tried all kinds of ways to get better, but the only way it happened was Jesus, Jesus, Jesus. Something about that name.

I wonder, why did John use seven miracles of Jesus to tell his story when we don't get to experience all those miracles ourselves? Do you know how many more children in our church I have prayed for and I haven't seen our requests granted the way we asked?

We wonder, why did Jesus heal some but not all?

I'll get to that. But let's look what the miracles do. I mean, they do something for those who experience the miracle, but what about those who see the miracles?

Jesus' miracles lead us to believe.

When Jesus turned the water into wine, John said it revealed Jesus' glory and the disciples believed in him (John 2:11). Jesus said, "Unless you people see signs and wonders . . . you will never believe" (4:48). He knows how we work.

When the official's son was healed, the whole family believed. Not believed he was healed—that was easy—they believed in Jesus (4:53).

When we see something that can't be explained, except by God, it leads to belief.

Jesus' miracles show us he can do anything.

This is what we find in John's progression of miracles.

Water into wine. Nicely done, Jesus! Cool party trick! I would have loved that one in college.

Then a sick boy's fever went away. This is getting serious.

The seventh miracle in John's gospel is dead Lazarus pulling off grave clothes, coming back to life (John 11). Whoa!

And John's last words of his book are "Jesus did many other things as well. If every one of them were written down . . . the whole world would not have room for the books" (21:25).

John intentionally shared seven miracles to show us that Jesus. Can. Do. Anything. There is just nothing Jesus can't do. But . . .

Jesus' miracles involve waiting and mystery, and they show us there is much we don't understand.

Miracles make any thinking person ask what we have already been asking ourselves. All the *where*, *what*, *who*, and *why* questions.

"Jesus, you turned water into wine. Where were you when I needed you?"

"Thirty-eight years that dude lay on the ground. Why didn't you show up thirty-seven years and eleven months earlier?"

"Why him, Jesus? Why not the other hundred people waiting on the water to be stirred?"

"Where were you when I cried out? Why wasn't that the right time? Why him and not me?"

Clearly the miracles of Jesus involve waiting and mystery, and there is much we don't understand. As I talked about in chapter 5, seeking clarity over certainty is the proper way; let's apply that here.

If we can't manipulate our way to hope, healing, and wholeness, and Jesus is our only hope for breaking open, and we are to look for miracles, but the miracles don't fit any neat plan of ours, then let's look at the questions.

Q: Where do miracles happen?
A: Anywhere. Wedding parties, little sick boys' bedrooms, street

corners where folks lie on the ground. *Anywhere. But we don't know where.*

Q: When do miracles happen?
A: Anytime. When we think our plan has run out, when all hope is lost, when we have waited so long we think it will never happen. *Anytime, but we don't know when.*

Q: So who gets the miracle? (That's a good question!)
A: Anyone. It can just be a spark to an already awesome party, or it can be for the one who has been forgotten for decades. Miracles happen for anyone. *Anyone, but we don't know who.*

We got a whopper of a miracle with Doug. His life is a miracle. He went to college and graduate school and became a counselor, back in the same town where his body was broken. Every day he sits with young people and shares hope, healing, and wholeness with others. He still walks with a limp. He still comes to our church. This fall I will officiate his wedding. Our church regularly celebrates his miracle. We stand and clap and cheer again. God did it!

But thirteen years after my first desperate prayer in the hospital lobby as a brand-new pastor, I am now well acquainted with that scene. I have sat in almost every gathering spot in Vanderbilt Medical Center's lobby with family after family. And I've encountered more mystery than certainty. The same year Doug was there I sat there with a large group of young adults, my high school friends. We got on our knees and prayed for our classmate's little girl Ava. What we asked for was not granted.

This is not any different from the people in Jesus' time. They would have reveled in the boy being healed, while others were not healed. They would have celebrated the miracle of the man thirty-eight years lame, while others still lay on the streets.

Do I believe in miracles? Oh yes I do. I do! I will pray it for you, ask for it, even claim it, but we will not think that we have the comprehension to understand how the eternal God works in all his ways.

Jesus' ultimate work is not a physical miracle. After every physical miracle that Jesus had the power and discretion to use, he would not allow people to focus on the physical. That's where we want to look, because that's what we can see. Instead, Jesus told people to pay attention to where he was going and where they were going. He says the same thing to us today.

John called Jesus' miracles *signs*. They pointed to something else. Jesus' miracles were pointing toward Jerusalem, to the cross, and to the empty grave.

With all the miracles Jesus worked and works, we see it is about way more than drinks at a party or even walking again. The miracles point to *the miracle* for everyone, everywhere, for all time.

All the miracles of our story are pointing to Jesus' miracle of life over death, which is our only hope. Crossing the Red Sea, the bread from heaven in the wilderness, the lion not eating Daniel, all these miracles of rescue were pointing to the rescue we will need. The miracles Jesus performed were all pointing. Jesus cares about physical things and provides physical healing, but it's not what it's all about. The ache that you and I feel is only met in him.

So we look for miracles because they point to Jesus. We resist manipulating our lives for fleeting pleasures and temporary satisfaction, and we are willing to break and suffer because it is in the breaking that we are made whole.

Again, where do miracles happen? Everywhere.

When do miracles happen? All the time.

Who gets the miracle? Everyone.

LIVE A LIFE EXPECTANT OF MIRACLES

Miracles happen in the presence of Jesus. In our marriages, with our kids, and, yes, in our sicknesses. We can't predict the timing of a miracle, but we can declare its coming. There is nothing too small, nothing too insignificant. It looks to me like Jesus worked a miracle to make his mom happy and delight some guests at a wedding (John 2). And there's nothing too big.

Let's summarize what this means for the one who is breaking open:

- *Look for miracles.* Are you looking? Not seeing any? Keep looking!

- *Ask for miracles.* Jesus' mother asked. She expected. The dad of the son asked. The paralyzed man told Jesus what he needed.

- *Pray for miracles.* We pray for miracles, not for a show or to manipulate others but because that is what we do in the presence of Jesus. We look. We ask. We pray.

- And this one: *Believe in miracles.* The miracles make us believe in Jesus and Jesus makes us believe in miracles. What another wonderful paradox.

We have already talked about belief. It involves some mystery. It involves faith. I believe that miracles are going to happen in your life, and we will be able to look back at this moment and say we asked and believed.

Some of us began reading this book with some places in us that were really broken. And as we come to the end of the last chapter, we still feel that brokenness. But with a miracle-working Jesus, we can reframe that brokenness in our lives. With a Jesus who experienced all the brokenness and then walked out of the grave whole, we are given an entirely new way to experience brokenness and an entirely new invitation to wholeness.

Paul called this "participation in his sufferings" (Philippians 3:10). He said we have to become like Jesus in his death. Christianity is founded on and is nothing without Jesus' resurrection. Easter is our day. But when Paul said that he wanted to know Christ, he said, "I want to know Christ—yes, to know the power of his resurrection

and participation in his sufferings, becoming like him in his death"
(v. 10, emphasis added).

Knowing Christ is power—the kind of power that leads you to walk out of the grave and gives you the ultimate healing that will be for now and all time.

Knowing Christ is also fully participating with the one who went to the cross, which allows us to look at the suffering we are in now as something that does not lack meaning. It is full of meaning. When our suffering is participating with Jesus, we are being broken in a different way: we break open. We know this is not the end.

Even as we feel like we are experiencing death in our lives, we can become like Jesus in his death—and for good reason. See how Paul finished his thought about knowing Christ.

"I want to know Christ—yes, to know the power of his resurrection and participation in his sufferings, becoming like him in his death, and so, somehow, attaining to the resurrection from the dead" (vv. 10–11).

So *somehow* attain to the resurrection from the dead. Well said, Paul. The great miracle is that somehow we get to live again. Be born again. Breathe again. It happens because Jesus poured himself out. And we participate with him when we pour ourselves out.

Our breaking moment right now will be the moment we look back on. We will point to the brokenness and say, "That was the moment

I came alive." It starts with a cry, but that cry gets our spiritual lungs going again.

The broken place is the setting for the miracle.

When *suicide* changed from just a word I had heard others talk about to a picture of a boy who had been my friend, when I ran away and Jesus chased me down, I broke. Open. I didn't know that the moment that felt like the end was actually the beginning. I didn't know that, as I felt like I was being crucified, I would come closer to the crucified one. And that, as I participated in his suffering, I was being ushered into power. The participation led to power.

That is a miracle. I have seen it. I have experienced it.

Jesus broke open so we could too.

I gave up on formulas to the perfect life and even formulas to the faithful life a long time ago. Life is messy. There is brokenness, and it comes at different times for different people. It's hard to fit what we experience here in real life on earth into any five steps or simple equations. But what I have outlined here in this book, I hope, is a pathway of sorts that you can walk on with Jesus and others.

It starts with slowing down our pace of life and finding space to breathe, laugh, love, live, and heal. Then we can rise out of the caves we've built to avoid enemies and enjoy good bread and wine. We can abandon self-focused drama and simply be really desperate for Jesus, Jesus, Jesus, Jesus.

This allows us to be less concerned about certainty and gain more clarity about Jesus' heart for us; he's the one who walks us through broken places. As we see him more clearly, we'll want to walk with him humbly. To pursue holiness and live like his set-apart people.

These steps leave us vulnerable, which opens us up to the *real life* God wants for us. Real relationships and real achievement, found in embracing who we are in Christ, not just what we are capable of doing.

Here, at last, we can release the controls on our lives (our attempts at control have been destructive anyway). We no longer have to manipulate each moment. Instead, we become aware of what Jesus is doing all around us and even participate in his life and death. We see miracles happening. And we trust in and for his miracles more than anything we could possibly manipulate.

But it's not just that we see miracles; our lives become miracles. Seeing our lives as miracles, we walk away from a life defined by the pain of our brokenness and into a whole new place—*a spacious place*, where God delights in us and offers intimate communion.

That's what I want to tell you about next.

It's the best part of breaking open.

A SPACIOUS PLACE

He reached down from on high and took hold
    of me;
he drew me out of deep waters.
He rescued me from my powerful enemy,
from my foes, who were too strong for me.
They confronted me in the day of my disaster,
but the Lord was my support.
He brought me out into a spacious place;
he rescued me because he delighted in me.

PSALM 18:16–19

A few years ago a particular phrase seemed to grab ahold of me: *a spacious place.*

It's really that phrase that got me writing this book. *A spacious place.* Not thinking about brokenness, not the ache, none of that. All these things were connected, of course, but what really got my attention was the promise. The promise from God that he would rescue.

The phrase was written by David, and it is found a few other places in the Bible. David wrote it when he was literally saved out of his enemy's hands. His enemy, Saul, had pursued David, but God was also pursuing David, and God miraculously saved him. So David wrote a song: "He brought me out into a spacious place; he rescued me because he delighted in me" (Psalm 18:19).

I realized that for me to get to a spacious place, it would be a rescue mission. Because I was running too fast, I was hunkered down in the cave—all the stuff we have been talking about. I had come to a place of being really tired. That's the best way to put it. But not tired like I need a day off. Not tired where vacation is the solution. I was so tired I needed a rescue.

Around that time our church, which had been meeting in a school for years, had just moved into our first permanent building. It was a glorious time. So many beautiful things had happened, and in many ways it was the culmination of a decade of working really hard toward a goal. On the third Sunday in the new building, I was standing in the lobby and a guy who had been on the ten-year journey with me approached and said, "This is great, huh?"

"Yeah," I said. And I meant it.

Then he asked, "So what's next?"

At first I wanted to punch him. *What do you mean, "What's next?" We just made it here.* But the next feeling was a strange one for me. I am a dreamer—a daydreamer, a nighttime dreamer. I love to dream. I love the future. That's my thing. And when he asked me "What's next?" the weird feeling I had was I didn't feel anything. I had nothing. I felt empty, with no dreams for the future.

That same afternoon, I went over to some friends' house for a meal, and there were a bunch of people there. It should have been a joyous time, but all I could feel was the feeling of nothingness that I had felt in the church lobby. My mind was clouded with nothing. It was weird. People were talking to me, but everyone sounded like Charlie Brown's teacher. I really felt like I couldn't hear their words. I went outside on the porch alone.

Now, please understand: I am well-versed in the panic attack. It wasn't that. I stood out there, kind of caught my breath, and cleaned out my ears. And it became clear to me what I was feeling. I was just really, really out of gas. I didn't need a nap or a day off. I needed a new way to live. I had let everything run out. I was on the verge of breakdown. I needed a rescue.

In my head that's when I heard the phrase *a spacious place*. David said, "He brought me out into a spacious place; he rescued me because he delighted in me." That phrase became my dream for the future. I wanted God to rescue me and set me in a spacious place. To get there, I would have to break open. I couldn't tough it out and get there. I had to let everything go and trust God.

That may be where you are right now. Just tired. Not dreaming anymore. Maybe you weren't even aware of the ache when you began reading this book. Now that you've made it this far with me in the book, do you want to pray a prayer together?

Let's do it.

> *God, we need you to rescue us. To rescue us from a powerful enemy. To set us in a spacious place and to delight in us there. Amen.*

I started reading through the Bible trying to note every place where there was some mention or vision of a spacious place. I found that all throughout the story God was rescuing broken, cramped, frantic people and first getting them in a place where there was some space to breathe, then meeting with them there.

But two places caught my attention—two places that were alike in so many ways, though separated by centuries. They were both spacious places where people who were breaking met with a God who desired to delight in them. Yet there is a distinct difference between the two stories: one ends with a breaking apart and the other ends with a breaking open.

The first is a garden in the beginning (Genesis 1–2). God had created, and he deemed the creation good. But when he worked another day and placed people in the creation, he called it "very good" (Genesis 1:31). On the day after that God stopped and set aside a day to be holy. A set-apart day when God stopped working and delighted in creation. God set apart this space, this day to be like no other day. It was holy.

God called the day holy and the time holy. The space was holy.

Then, what God had made holy experienced brokenness. Devastation. The man and woman who were able to walk with a God who delighted in them in this garden threw it all away. They chose to take control. They valued capability above vulnerability. They sought to manipulate life to their advantage, just like we all have.

It was a breakdown of epic proportions. Sin entered in the garden and the people were expelled. There is no mention of crying, but it's hard for me to imagine that Adam and Eve did not weep, wail, and moan as they walked out of the spacious place God had created to the cramped, exhausting, broken world outside. Tears in the garden.

I began this book with a story of my own devastation that also included for me a redemptive moment, the birth of my daughter Mary. She was born one year to the day after my greatest loss.

When Mary was born I was a full-time student attending a university one hour from our home. I would go to school early in the morning, make the commute back, go to work, and usually return home later in the evening. I was gone all day, and we had little Mary. So even though it was big-time against our sleep-training rules, every morning, while it was still dark before I left for school, I would sneak into Mary's room and whisper to this tiny baby.

"Mary."

Then a bit louder, "Mary."

And she would open her eyes.

When she opened her eyes, I would snatch her up and then simply rock her back to sleep, saying her name. She'd close her eyes; I'd put her back in the crib and go to school.

I performed that morning ritual because I wanted her to know me. I wanted her to know her name, but I wanted her to know the way her name sounded coming from my voice. It was a spacious place where I would delight in her. I'm sure Mary can't remember those moments, but I hope they are imprinted on her heart.

We have had other moments where the evidence of those early morning "Marys" have shown me that she does indeed know what her name sounds like coming from my voice. There was the time she fell face-first into the dirt at third base when I was coaching her softball team. I was able to raise her up out of that embarrassment by saying "Mary." Her head twitched up to attention. It was an instinct for her to react to her name from my voice. We had practiced it thousands of times beforehand. "Mary, run home," I said. The catcher had missed the throw from right field. So she got up and ran with all of her might, scoring the run, and turned back to me with a ponytail bobbing under her helmet and a big grin on her face.

More recently there have been late nights when I have called her—she is fine, but I am worried—and when she answers the phone, I say "Mary," and she knows it's me.

We have so much life packed into seventeen years now with me saying her name and her knowing it's me.

The second spacious place in the Bible I mentioned is also a garden, and this event also takes place very early in the morning. Easter morning—which happened "early on the first day of the week, while it was still dark" (John 20:1).

The character who came into the garden was Mary Magdalene. She was one of Jesus' friends, one of Jesus' followers, one of Jesus' disciples. She is mentioned eleven times in the four accounts of Jesus' life, which is way more than most of the disciples. She is an important figure. We are told that Jesus cast seven devils out of her (Mark 16:9). Mary was with Jesus on his journeys, she was there as he hung on the cross, and she was there in the garden at Jesus' tomb.

You probably know the story: the tomb was empty. Now we find joy in the empty tomb—we sing songs about it. "An empty tomb lets us know our Savior lives."[1] But that's not what an empty tomb meant to Mary. To her, an empty tomb meant, *Oh, God, you have to be kidding me. It's worse than I thought*. An empty tomb was cause for a breakdown.

Mary told Peter and John about the empty tomb; they came and looked, then returned home. But Mary stayed at the tomb. She stayed and she cried. Tears in the garden.

Mary sensed someone was behind her.

Jesus was there. God was walking in the garden again.

But Mary didn't realize it was Jesus. He looked so different, or her vision was so clouded by tears, she thought Jesus must be the gardener.

The supposed gardener said, "Mary."

There might have been a lot of crazy stuff going on—she might have been mid-breakdown—but Mary did not mistake the sound of her name coming from his voice. She'd heard it too many times. She knew Jesus. She knew the way he said her name. And now, she knew Jesus was not dead. Not anymore. He was alive.

Jesus announced his resurrection—his universe-shaking, world-changing resurrection—by saying the name of his friend.

The beginning of new creation.

In a garden.

Where tears were falling.

This was the moment when Jesus revealed that, because of his suffering on the cross and empty tomb, *people could be saved.* When he said "Mary" he was also saying, "I've rescued you."

We can't give up.

Today we may be grieving the loss of a friend, an illness, an opportunity that won't come back. A marriage that is toast. A regret we can't let go of. But we can't give up. We can't stop looking for the miracle. Mary had seven devils. How many do you have? Jesus can drive them away. *How?* you might ask. *How can Jesus do that for me?*

I don't know exactly, but I know that he can wake up a dead heart and make it come alive again. I've learned it usually involves tears. There is a breaking. But the breaking doesn't have to lay us low. In fact, the breaking can be the thing that opens us to life again.

I believe Jesus had the power to sit up in his grave and carefully take his bandages off, neatly pile them on the floor, and then bust out of a cave.

The breaking open of the tomb is the picture of what God can do for you when you break open.

That God, who has that power, desires to rescue you.

To delight in you.

He knows your stinking name.

So let the tears kickstart your heart back to life through the power of the one who participates in our suffering and is resurrected from the grave.

Break, yes—but *break open*.

ACKNOWLEDGMENTS

Thank you to . . .

Rachel—I love you with everything I've got. All my stories are really our stories. My heart is most full when I am with you. Thanks for jumping off the dock under the strawberry moon. That was epic.

Mary, Lydia, and Phoebe—Your births changed my life; but really, it's your lives that have changed my life. Hog shows, the Coke museum, listening to Taylor Swift (incessantly)—all of it and all of you have made my life abundant and fun. Remember when Mom jumped into the lake? Epic.

Providence Church—You have given me the space to learn and grow as a pastor and teacher (from my twenties to now in my forties!). You have loved me so well. You walked with me through my breaking moments and gave grace upon grace. I am grateful.

Providence Church pastors and staff—I can't believe we get to do what we do together. So much hope, healing, and wholeness right before our eyes. Thank you for your support and forgiveness and laughter and tears.

Samantha—Thank you for your support, patience, attention to detail, and every e-mail I get from you that says, "This is complete."

My band of brothers—Mark, Bryan, Chip, Ryan, Lee, and Travis. Your prayers and friendship have steadied me through all our breaking and healing.

The Sanctification Project—Jorge, Dale, Craig, Ron, Jim, Mike, Travis, Matthew, and Wes. Our weekly iron-sharpening-iron has given me fuel for our passion . . . to make disciples who make disciples.

Nick—Thank you for patiently counseling me and reminding me that pain can hold the path to living again.

Andrew Peterson—Thank you for carrying me along on your songs for the last twenty years. For reminding me to wait on the sun; it is indeed darkest just before the dawn.

W Publishing—Damon Reiss, for believing in me and making me laugh. Carrie Marrs, for taking what I wrote and making it better and better and better. To both of you for praying that God would use my words for good. The whole team has been incredible to me. Thank you.

And . . .

Jesus, Jesus, Jesus, Jesus. You are everything and everything to me. I can't wait to hear you say my name.

NOTES

Chapter 1: Breaking Open, Not Breaking Down
1. Paul Simon, "Gumboots," *Graceland*, Warner Records, 1986.
2. Paul Simon, "Gumboots."
3. Timothy J. Keller, "Hope for the World," Gospel in Life, September 27, 2009, 13:31, MP3 audio, https://gospelinlife.com /downloads/hope-for-the-world-6022/.

Chapter 2: Space, Not Pace
1. C. Austin Miles, "In the Garden" (1913), Hymnary.org, https:// hymnary.org/text/i_come_to_the_garden_alone.
2. Okay, they did. Definitely read John Townsend and Henry Cloud's *Boundaries* (Grand Rapids: Zondervan, 1992).

Chapter 3: Rising Up, Not Hunkering Down

1. C. J. Ellicott, *Ellicott's Commentary for English Readers* (London: Cassell and Co., 1897), https://biblehub.com/commentaries /ellicott/judges/6.htm; G. F. Maclear, *Cambridge Bible for Schools and Colleges* (Cambridge, England: Cambridge University Press, 1897), https://biblehub.com/commentaries/cambridge/judges /6.htm.
2. "Coca-Cola Life Arrives on Shelves Nationwide," Coca-Cola Company, November 3, 2014, https://www.coca-colacompany .com/news/coca-cola-life-launches-nationwide.
3. *The Princess Bride*, directed by Rob Reiner, featuring Cary Elwes, Robin Wright, Mandy Patinkin, Chris Sarandon (Burbank, CA: Twentieth Century Fox, 1987), DVD, 1:38.

Chapter 4: Desperate, Not Dramatic

1. This story is adapted from Jacob Armstrong, *A New Playlist* (Nashville: Abingdon Press, 2018), 37–38.
2. Richard J. Foster, *Celebration of Discipline* (San Francisco: Harper and Row, 1988), 60.
3. Moses, Exodus 34:28; David, 2 Samuel 12:16; Elijah, 1 Kings 19; Esther, Esther 4; Daniel, Daniel 10:2–3; Anna, Luke 2:36–38; Paul, Acts 9:9; Jesus, Matthew 4.
4. Dallas Willard, *The Spirit of the Disciplines* (San Francisco: Harper and Row, 1988), 166.

Chapter 6: Holiness, Not Haughtiness

1. John Wesley, quoted in Kevin Watson, *Perfect Love* (Franklin, TN: Seedbed Publishing, 2021), 101–17. For more on sanctification, check out this masterful book.

Chapter 7: Vulnerability, Not Capability

1. "Vital Signs," Cleveland Clinic, January 23, 2019, https:// my.clevelandclinic.org/health/articles/10881-vital-signs; Adam Rowden, "What Is a Normal Respiratory Rate Based on

Your Age?," Medical News Today, December 21, 2021, https://www.medicalnewstoday.com/articles/324409#adults. Articles like these give a range of what number of breaths per minute is normal for adults; I've seen between 12 to 20 breaths per minute, so I landed on "about 15 times." I then used the rate of 15 breaths per minute to estimate how many times during the chapter (20 minutes), and to get around 23,000 times per day (1,440 minutes), and the year and lifetime numbers.

2. Abraham, Genesis 26:24; Moses, Numbers 21:34; Elijah, 2 Kings 1:15; Mary, Luke 1:30; Joseph, Matthew 1:20.

3. Stephen B. Oates, *Let the Trumpet Sound: A Life of Martin Luther King Jr.* (New York: Harper and Row, 1982), 88.

4. Oates, *Trumpet*, 88.

5. Oates, 88–89.

6. Oates, 89.

7. This story is told in Jacob Armstrong, *God's Messy Family* (Nashville: Abingdon Press, 2018), 52–53.

Conclusion: A Spacious Place

1. Bill Gaither, "Because He Lives," *A Billy Graham Music Homecoming*, Spring House, 2001.

ABOUT THE
AUTHOR

Jacob Armstrong lives in Mt. Juliet, Tennessee, with his wife, Rachel, and their three daughters, Mary, Lydia, and Phoebe. He is the pastor of Providence Church, a church that is committed to seeing those who feel disconnected from God and the church find hope, healing, and wholeness in Jesus Christ. Jacob has a master's degree from the University of the South School of Theology and is the author of ten books and studies, including *The New Adapters*, *God's Messy Family*, and *A New Playlist*. To hear more of Jacob's teachings, go to www.prov.church.